SO-CFL-472

Country Furniture
Cupboards, Cabinets, and Shelves

Collected and Written
by Nick Engler

Rodale Press
Emmaus, Pennsylvania

If you have any questions or comments concerning this book, please write:

Rodale Press
Book Reader Service
33 East Minor Street
Emmaus, PA l8098

Series Editor: Jeff Day
Managing Editor/Author: Nick Engler
Editor: Roger Yepsen
Copy Editor: Mary Green
Graphic Designer: Linda Watts
Graphic Artists: Mary Jane Favorite
                 Chris Walendzak
Photography: Karen Callahan
Cover Photography: Mitch Mandel
Cover Photograph Stylist: Janet C. Vera
Proofreader: Hue Park
Typesetting by Computer Typography, Huber Heights, Ohio
Interior Illustrations by O'Neil & Associates, Dayton, Ohio
Endpaper Illustrations by Mary Jane Favorite
Produced by Bookworks, Inc., West Milton, Ohio

Library of Congress Cataloging-in-Publication Data
Engler, Nick.
    Country furniture: cupboards, cabinets, and shelves/
collected and written by Nick Engler.
        p.   cm.—(Build-it-better-yourself woodworking
      projects)
    ISBN 0–87857–929–X   hardcover
    ISBN 0–87857–953–2   paperback
    1. Cabinet-work.   2. cupboards.   3. Shelving (Furniture)
4. Country furniture.   I. Title.   II. Series: Engler, Nick. Build-it-better-yourself woodworking projects.
TT197.E529   1990
684. 1′6—dc20   90–35898
                                                  CIP

Distributed in the book trade by St. Martin's Press

2 4 6 8 10 9 7 5 3 1 hardcover
2 4 6 8 10 9 7 5 3 1 paperback

Contents

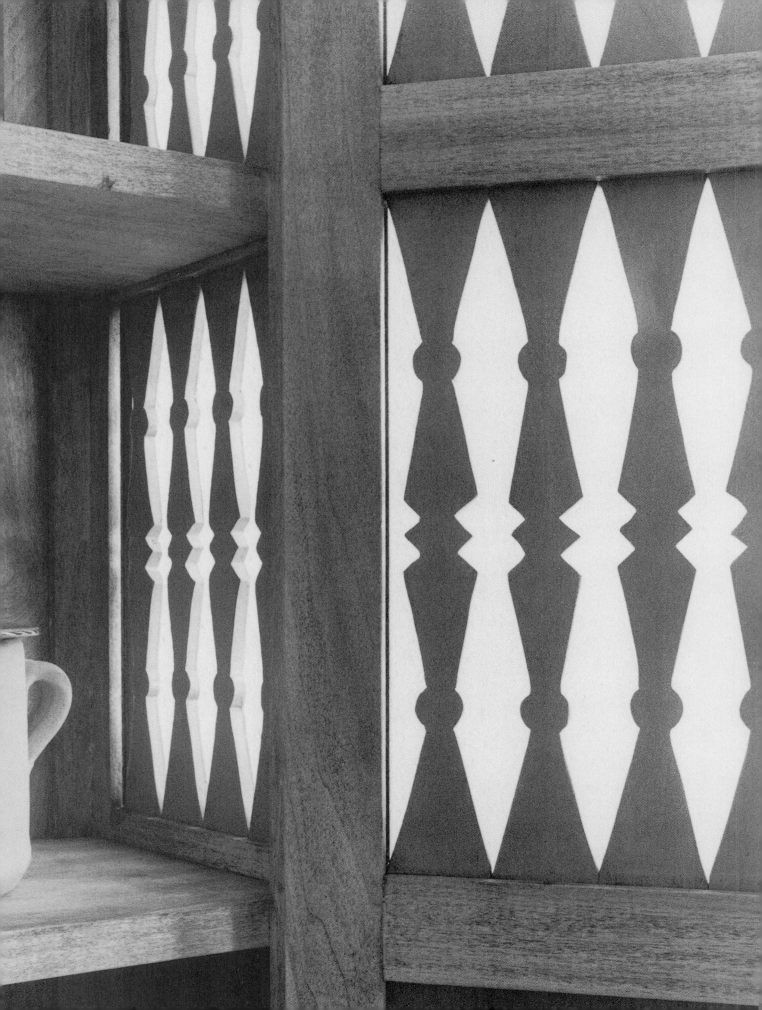

Survival of the Useful

Each generation develops its own furniture needs and tastes. Folks choose the most practical forms and styles from the previous generation, add their own refinements, and discard the rest. In some cases, they invent new forms by combining or modifying old ones to make them more functional or elegant. Useful furniture survives. Those forms that have outlived their usefulness are retired to attics or museums.

You can see evolution at work in the development of cupboards and cabinets from simple shelves.

Shelves

Before the Renaissance, ordinary country homes were barren of furniture, beyond a few primitive stools and tables. Although wood was plentiful, boards were costly. They either had to be "riven" from logs (split with a wedge), or laboriously produced with a pit saw. As a result, only the very rich had even the crudest furniture. Most of the surfaces that common folk needed for eating, sitting, working, and sleeping were incorporated into the architecture of a house — built into the walls.

In the fourteenth century, two important things happened that changed this forever. First, there was a protracted period of relative peace, in which trade and agriculture prospered. Cities grew, and a middle class appeared. These people had enough money that they could contemplate buying something as luxurious as a piece of furniture. Then, in 1328, the first water-powered sawmill was built in Germany. As the invention spread throughout Europe, boards — and furniture — were suddenly much easier to come by.

Among the first pieces of furniture to appear in ordinary homes were shelves. They were useful, versatile, and simple to build. They would hold almost anything and could be hung or set anywhere. And, for a time, "dressers" (shelves that held dinnerware) were very stylish. Both the dressers and the dinnerware were visible proof of prosperity. Furthermore, the number of shelves in a dresser was a symbol of station. The French ambassador to England once gave King Henry VIII a dresser with 12 shelves.

Cupboards

As Europe continued to prosper, shelves evolved into another useful form. Renaissance "joiners" (woodworkers) fastened doors to the old dressers, making what we now call cupboards. (Originally, the word "cupboard" referred to a much simpler piece. It was a single shelf or *board* set into a wall to hold *cups* and other dinnerware.) The cupboard doors kept the dust and dirt off the dishes. This was an important innovation, since many country homes still had dirt floors.

Folks didn't discard their open shelves, however. Not every household item needed to be stored in an enclosed space — it was a nuisance to open and close cupboard doors to retrieve frequently used items. Craftsmen combined the two forms, building pieces with cupboards on the bottom and shelves on top. Furniture with two types of storage — open and enclosed — was doubly useful. This design became the classic hutch or dish dresser.

Cabinets

In the sixteenth century, Europe began to import fine porcelain from the Orient. Folks wanted to display these treasures — put them in a protective enclosure, yet still be able to see them. To allow this, joiners developed a cupboard with glass doors. The French called this a *cabinette* (which the English shortened to "cabinet"), after the word *cabin,* a one-room house with windows.

Because of the sash work (sash rails, stiles, and glazing bars) needed to hold the glass, cabinets were more difficult to make than shelves or cupboards. Joiners who possessed the required skills advertised themselves as "cabinetmakers." The term quickly became synonymous with makers of fine furniture.

Once again, folks didn't discard their shelves or cupboards for the newly evolved cabinets. Each form was useful for a particular type of storage, and several could be combined to serve different needs. And all three forms survive today because of their continued utility.

Santa Fe Wall Cupboard

In 1521, when the Spanish conquered New Spain — the area we know as Mexico, California, Arizona, and New Mexico — they found that many of the natives in the area were highly skilled woodworkers. In particular, the Pueblos and their neighbors in New Mexico had a rich woodworking tradition.

As part of the Spanish missionary efforts, immigrant *ensembladores* (cabinetmakers) taught the enslaved Indians to reproduce European furniture. The Indians found that the geometric designs of the Spanish were similar to their own design customs, and began to mix the two. By the seventeenth century, Indian and *mestizo* (Indian-Spanish) craftsmen were making country pieces in their own style. An example is this lattice-work cupboard or *trastero*. These Indian-Spanish furniture designs developed for almost three centuries in the mission towns of the Southwest, particularly in Albuquerque and Santa Fe.

A distinctive aspect of the *Southwest* style, as it came to be called, was that the pieces were highly decorated — much more so than most eastern country furniture. Craftsmen spent countless hours making moldings, fretwork, lattice, carvings, and painted designs. This cupboard includes all five of these decorative techniques. The stiles and rails are molded, and the top rails have fretwork shapes. The splats form an intricate lattice. The panels and the front stiles have carved grooves or triangles. Finally, the splats and top rails are painted with designs.

Another distinction is that most of these decorations are geometric. When Spain was occupied by the Moslem Moors in the eighth century, the Spanish adopted their geometric design motifs, called *mujedar*. The Aztec and Pueblo Indians developed a remarkably similar style of decoration long before the Spanish conquest. These two geometric decorative customs, Islamic and Indian, combine to make a unique style in Southwest country furniture.

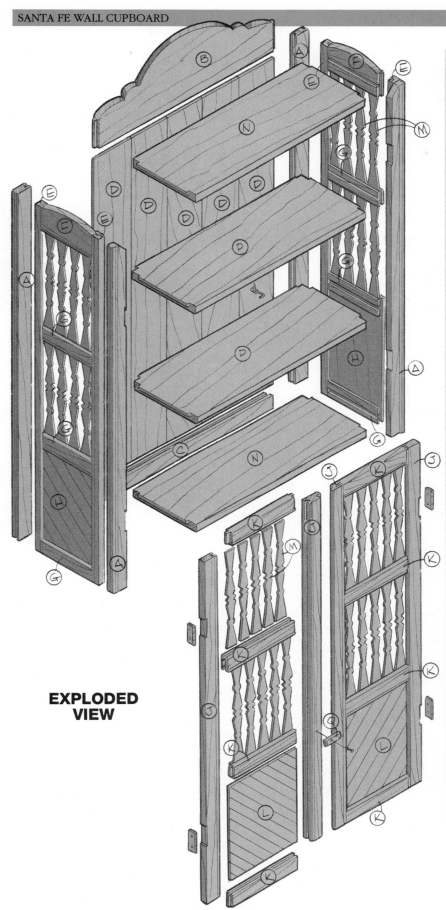

EXPLODED VIEW

Materials List

FINISHED DIMENSIONS

PARTS

A. Front/back
stiles (4)   3/4″ x 1 1/2″ x 37″

B. Top back rail   3/4″ x 7″ x 21 1/4″

C. Bottom back rail   3/4″ x 1 1/2″ x 21 1/4″

D. Backboards   1/4″ x (variable)
(4 or 5)   x 33 3/16″

E. Side stiles (4)   3/4″ x 3/4″ x 37″

F. Top side rails (2)   3/4″ x 3″ x 6 3/4″

G. Middle/bottom
side rails (6)   3/4″ x 1 1/2″ x 6 3/4″

H. Side panels (2)   1/4″ x 6 5/8″ x 10 11/16″

J. Door stiles (4)   3/4″ x 1 1/2″ x 36″

K. Door rails (8)   3/4″ x 1 1/2″ x 8 1/4″

L. Door panels (2)   1/4″ x 8 1/8″ x 10 11/16″

M. Lattice
splats (36)   1/4″ x 1 1/2″ x 10 11/16″

N. Top/bottom
shelves (2)   3/4″ x 7 1/2″ x 22 1/2″

P. Middle
shelves (2)   3/4″ x 7 3/4″ x 22 1/2″

Q. Latch   1/2″ x 1″ x 2″

HARDWARE

#8 x 1 1/4″ Flathead wood screw
5/8″ Wire brads (1 box)
1 1/2″ x 2″ Butt hinges and mounting
screws (2 pairs)
Small hook and eye

1 Select the stock and cut the parts to size.
To make this project, you need about 16 board feet of 4/4 (four-quarters) lumber and 4 board feet of 8/4 (eight-quarters) lumber. The wall cupboard shown is made from ponderosa pine — Southwest craftsmen worked almost exclusively with this wood.

Resaw 4 board feet of 4/4 lumber in half, and plane it to $\frac{1}{4}''$ thick. Plane the remaining 4/4 stock to $\frac{3}{4}''$. Thickness the 8/4 stock to $1\frac{1}{2}''$. Cut the parts to the sizes shown in the Materials List, except the backboards and splats.

2 Cut the frame and panel joinery.
The parts of this cupboard are all assembled with tongue-and-groove joints and rabbets. Using a table-mounted router or dado cutter, cut the joints in this order:

- $\frac{1}{4}''$-wide, $\frac{3}{8}''$-deep grooves in the inside edges of the stiles, top rails, and bottom rails
- $\frac{1}{4}''$-wide, $\frac{3}{8}''$-deep grooves in both edges of all middle rails (both side and front), as shown in the *Middle Side Rail Layout*
- $\frac{1}{4}''$-thick, $\frac{3}{8}''$-long tongues in the ends of all the rails

- $\frac{3}{8}''$-wide, $\frac{1}{4}''$-deep grooves in the inside faces of the bottom and middle side rails, $\frac{9}{16}''$ from the bottom edges
- $\frac{3}{8}''$-wide, $\frac{3}{8}''$-deep grooves in the inside faces of the side top rails, $1\frac{1}{8}''$ from the bottom edges, as shown in the pattern for them
- $\frac{3}{8}''$-thick, $\frac{1}{4}''$-long tongues in the ends of the shelves, as shown in the *Shelf Layouts*
- $\frac{3}{8}''$-wide, $\frac{3}{8}''$-deep rabbets in the outside edges of the inside door rails, as shown in *Section A*

3 Cut and fit the backboards.
Dry assemble the back rails and stiles. Cut the backboards to length, and rip them to random widths — $3''$–$6''$. Slide the backboards into their grooves, and rip the last one to fit. When lined up edge to edge, the backboards should form a panel $33\frac{3}{16}''$ tall and $22\frac{3}{4}''$ wide, with $\frac{1}{16}''$ gaps between the boards.

4 Cut the notches in the shelves.
The shelves are notched to fit into the side assemblies and against the back assembly. Lay out the notches, as shown in the *Shelf Layouts,* and cut them with a band saw or saber saw.

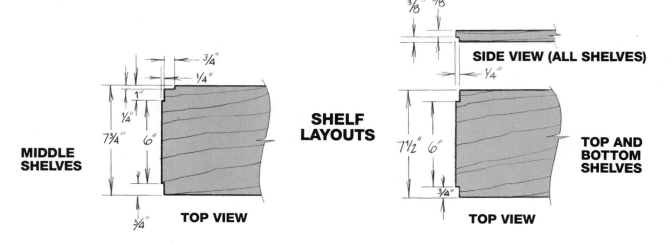

SHELF LAYOUTS

MIDDLE SHELVES — TOP VIEW

SIDE VIEW (ALL SHELVES)

TOP AND BOTTOM SHELVES — TOP VIEW

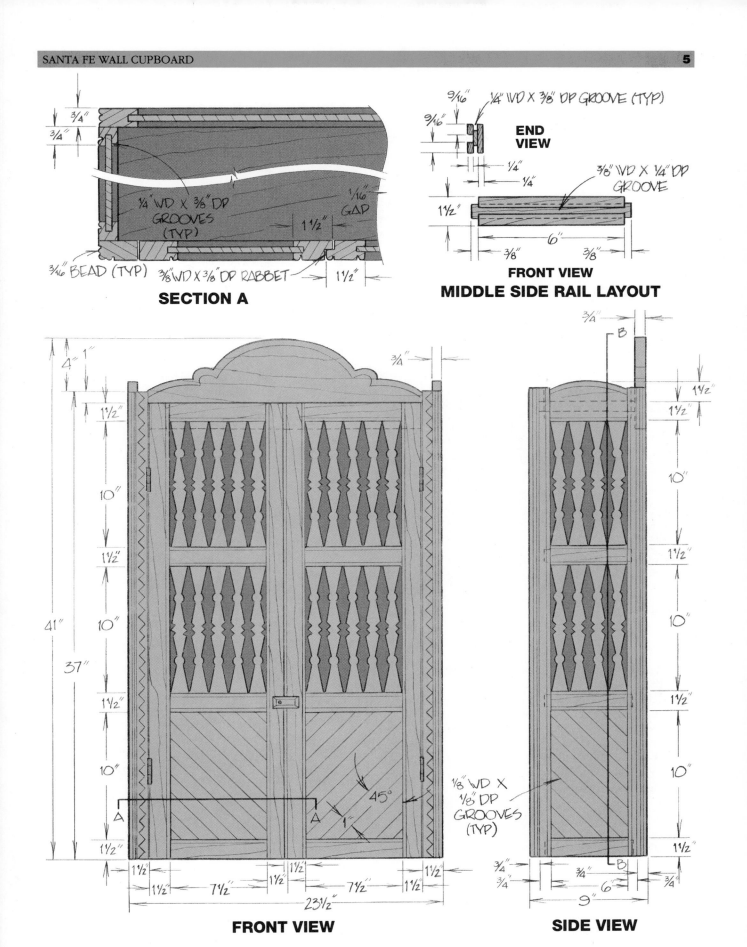

SECTION A

FRONT VIEW
MIDDLE SIDE RAIL LAYOUT

FRONT VIEW

SIDE VIEW

5 **Cut the shapes of the top rails.** Enlarge the *Top Back Rail Pattern* and *Top Side Rail Pattern*. Trace these on the stock, then cut them out with a band saw or saber saw. Sand the sawed edges to remove the saw marks.

Drill two ¼"-diameter holes through the top back rail, near the bottom edge, as shown in *Section B*. The spacing of these holes is not critical, as long as they are 12" apart or more. Later, you can use these holes to mount the cupboard on a wall.

6 **Cut the shapes of the splats.** Cut the 1½"-thick stock into several blocks 10¹¹/₁₆" long and 4"–5" wide. Enlarge the *Splat Pattern* and trace it on one edge of each block. Cut the shapes with a band saw, then sand the sawed surfaces. Slice the blocks into ¼" splats on a table saw. (See Figures 1 and 2.)

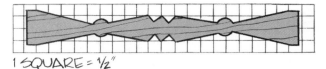

1 SQUARE = ½"

SPLAT PATTERN

1/To save yourself the trouble of having to make 36 individual splats, first saw the shape in the edge of a thick board. Sand the sawed surfaces smooth.

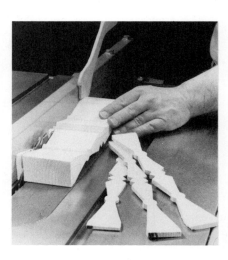

2/Slice the thick board into narrow strips, as shown. Each strip will form a shaped splat. **Sawguard removed for clarity.**

7 **Cut the beads in the rails and stiles.** To add decoration to the frame members, each of them has one or more ³/₁₆" beads in the outside surface. Old-time Indian craftsmen made these beads with a hand tool called a "scratch stock." You can make them with a molder and three-bead knives. Or, use a table-mounted router and a point-cut quarter-round bit:

- Cut single beads near the inside edges of the side stiles, outside door stiles, left inside door stile, top side rails, top door rails, bottom side rails, and bottom door rails.
- Cut single beads near both edges of the middle side rails and right inside door stile. (See Figure 3.)
- Cut double beads in the outside edges of the back stiles. (See Figure 4.)
- Cut double beads in the outside edges *and* outside faces of the front stiles. These two cuts should overlap, so there are just three beads at each front corner. (See Figure 5.)

3/Cut single ³/₁₆" beads in the outside surface of the middle side rails. Make one bead near each edge, as shown. If you're using a molder and three-bead knives, cover two of the beads with a wooden fence.

4/Cut two ³/₁₆″ beads in the outside edges of the back stiles. If you're using three-bead knives to make these shapes, simply move the fence over to expose another bead.

5/Cut two ³/₁₆″ beads in the outside edges **and** the outside surfaces of the front stiles. These beads should overlap at the corners.

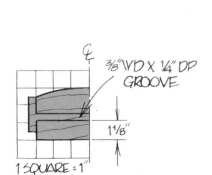

³/₈″ WD X ¼″ DP GROOVE

1¹/₈″

1 SQUARE = 1″

TOP SIDE RAIL PATTERN

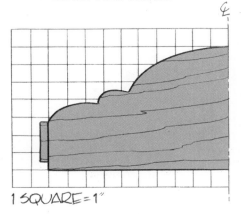

1 SQUARE = 1″

TOP BACK RAIL PATTERN

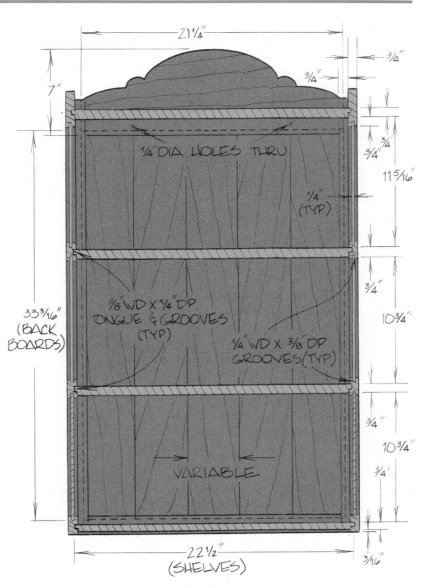

21¼″

7″

³/₄″

³/₄″

¼″ DIA HOLES THRU

³/₄″

³/₄″

11⁵/₁₆″

¼″ (TYP)

33³/₁₆″ (BACK BOARDS)

³/₈″ WD X ¼″ DP TONGUE & GROOVES (TYP)

³/₄″

10³/₄″

¼″ WD X ³/₈″ DP GROOVES (TYP)

³/₄″

VARIABLE

10³/₄″

³/₄″

22½″ (SHELVES)

³/₁₆″

SECTION B

8. Miter the front stiles.

Miter the front stiles. The top corners of the front stiles slope toward one another for aesthetic effect. Miter the top inside corners of the front stiles at 45°, as shown in the *Front Stile Top End Detail*. Sand the sawed edges.

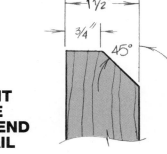

FRONT STILE TOP END DETAIL

9. Cut grooves in the panels and front stiles.

Cut grooves in the panels and front stiles. The panels all have decorative grooves in the outside surfaces. Cut these grooves at a 45° angle, using an ordinary table saw blade. Cut the grooves in the right and left side panels so they slope toward the bottom back corners; the grooves in the right and left door panels slope toward the bottom inside cor□ The spacing of these grooves isn't critical, but th□ should be fairly even.

If you wish, you can also cut grooves in the fro□ with a chisel. These grooves should form a zigz□ tern, as shown in the *Front View*.

10. Paint the splats and panels.

Paint the splats and panels. As shown in the lead photograph, both the splats and the panels are painted while the rest of the cupboard is finished naturally. The splats are painted with simple designs, and the panels are painted a single color. Before painting, finish sand the splats and panels. Then, if you wish, paint these parts with *pastel* colors or earth tones. For help in choosing these colors, consult books on Southwest country furniture. Here are two p□ titles that you may be able to get from your local□ or through inter-library loan:

■ *Santa Fe Style,* by Christine Mather and Sha□ Woods (New York: Rizzoli, 1986)
■ *New Mexican Furniture 1600–1940,* by Lo□ Taylor and Dessa Bokides (Santa Fe: Museu□ New Mexico Press, 1987)

11. Assemble the frames and panels.

Assemble the frames and panels. Finish sand the remaining parts. Glue the rails to the stiles, inserting the tenons in the grooves. Place the backboards, splats, and panels in their appropriate grooves, but do *not* glue them in place. These parts must float in the grooves.

Reinforce the tongue-and-groove joints with wire brads. Drive the brads through the back surface of the stiles and into the rails. Use two brads per joint. (See Figure 6.)

6/To pin each tongue-and-groove joint together, drive two ⅝" wire brads through the stiles and into the rails from the inside surface. Set the heads of the brads, but be careful the points of the brads don't protrude on the outside surface.

Position the splats so they line up in the frames. The outside edges of the right and left splats should be visible; these splats should rest in the rail grooves *only*. They mustn't be partially hidden in the stile grooves. Drive single brads through the rails and into the right or left splats, as shown in the *Splat Detail*. This will keep the splats from shifting in their grooves.

Set the heads of the brads slightly below the surface, then sand all joints clean and flush.

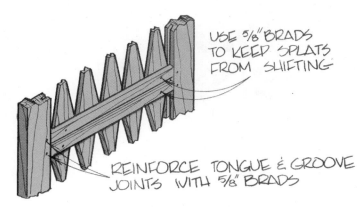

USE 5/8" BRADS TO KEEP SPLATS FROM SHIFTING

REINFORCE TONGUE & GROOVE JOINTS WITH 5/8" BRADS

SPLAT DETAIL
INSIDE VIEW

12 Assemble the case. Glue the back assembly, side assemblies, front stiles, and shelves together. Glue the shelves to the front, back, and side stiles, but *not* to the side rails. Simply insert the shelf tongues in the rail grooves. Sand all joints clean and flush.

13 Mount the doors. Mortise the front stiles and outside door stiles for hinges, then mount the doors to the case. Install a hook and eye inside the case to keep the left door closed, as shown in the *Door Keeper Detail*.

With a sander or a file, chamfer the ends and edges of the latch, as shown in the *Latch Details*. Drill a 1/8"-diameter pilot hole through the latch, and countersink the hole. Attach the latch to the left door, even with the lower middle door rails, using the flathead screw. The position of the latch is shown in the *Front View*.

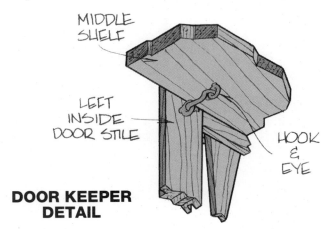

MIDDLE SHELF

LEFT INSIDE DOOR STILE

HOOK & EYE

DOOR KEEPER DETAIL

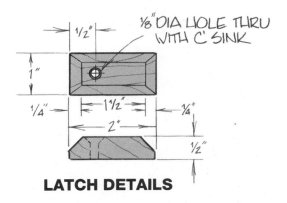

1/2"

1"

1/4"

1 1/2"

2"

1/4"

1/2"

1/8" DIA HOLE THRU WITH C'SINK

LATCH DETAILS

14 Apply a finish to the cupboard. Remove the doors, latch, and hardware from the case. Do any necessary touch-up sanding. Then, if you wish, paint the top edges of the top back rail and top side rails. Apply a stain or a natural finish to the completed cupboard, inside and out. Put the stain right over the paint — this will soften the colors, making them look aged. Let the finish dry. Replace the doors, latch, and hardware.

Whale-End Shelves

To add decoration to racks and shelves, country craftsmen often cut various shapes in the vertical supports. Some of these contours were simple geometric patterns. Others mimicked the prevailing furniture styles or incorporated traditional folk patterns. Still others were flights of individual fancy.

During the Queen Anne period — the mid-eighteenth century — craftsmen began to incorporate flowing S-curves (also called cyma curves or "ogees") into their furniture designs. This shelving unit is one example. Narrow, hanging shelves with ogee supports became very popular during the period, and continued to be made into the early nineteen called shelves tinctive silhoue whales differe space b a differ

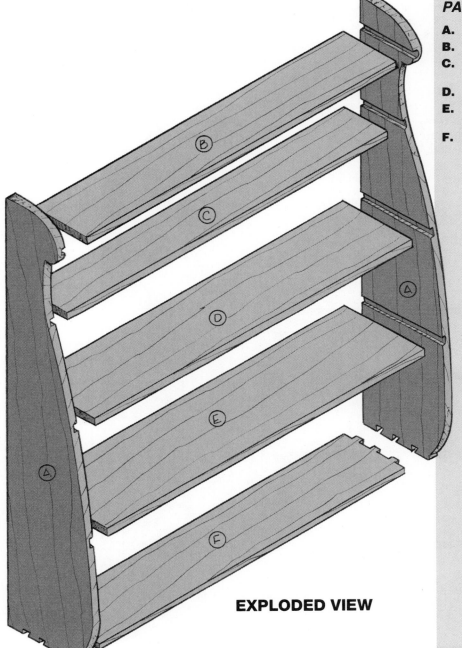

EXPLODED VIEW

Materials List

FINISHED DIMENSIONS

PARTS

A. Sides (2) $5/8''$ x $8^3/8''$ x 38"

B. Top shelf $7/16''$ x $5^3/8''$ x $31^1/2''$

C. Top middle shelf $7/16''$ x $3^7/8''$ x $31^1/2''$

D. Middle shelf $7/16''$ x $5^{15}/16''$ x $31^1/2''$

E. Bottom middle shelf $7/16''$ x $7^1/2''$ x $31^1/2''$

F. Bottom shelf $7/16''$ x $6^3/4''$ x 32"

HARDWARE

4d Square-cut nails (20)

1

Select the stock and cut the parts to size. To build these shelves, you'll need about 13 board feet of 4/4 (four-quarters) lumber. The whale-end shelves shown are made from walnut, but country craftsmen might have also used cherry or figured maple. A few were made from chestnut and elm. If they planned to paint the finishe[...] might have used poplar or white pine.

Plane about 3 board feet to ⁵⁄₈" thick, [...] der to ⁷⁄₁₆" thick. Cut the sides and the b[...] the sizes shown in the Materials List. Rip [...] shelves about ⅛" wider than specified.

2

Cut the dadoes in the sides. All the shelves except the bottom shelf are dadoed to the sides. The bottom shelf is dovetailed. Using a router or a dado blade, cut ⁷⁄₁₆"-wide, ³⁄₈"-deep [...] side stock, as shown in the *Side View*.

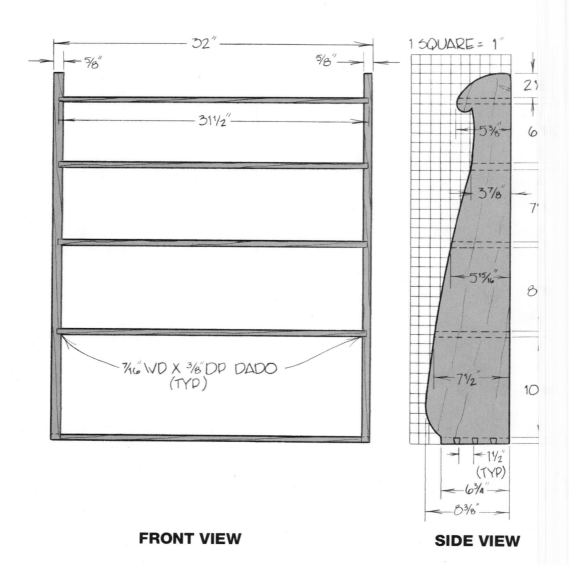

FRONT VIEW

SIDE VIEW

6 he dovetail joints. As mentioned, the bottom shelf joins the sides with "through" dovetails. There are several commercial router jigs that will cut through dovetails, or you can make them by hand, following the procedure shown in Figures 1 through 10.

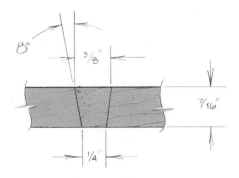

DOVETAIL DETAIL

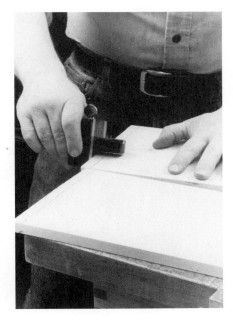

*1/Start with either the pins or the tails — most craftsmen prefer the tails. Using a marking gauge, scribe two lines — one on each face — near the end of the board. These lines indicate the length of the tails, and are called **baselines**.*

*2/Using an awl or knife, scribe the sides or "cheeks" of the tails on **both** sides of the board. Make a T-shaped jig to lay out and cut the dovetails. Angle the applied faces of the "T" to match the dovetails. Later, you can use this jig to guide the saw.*

*3/Saw the cheeks of the tails down to the baselines, cutting on the waste side of the marks. Use a small, fine-toothed saw, such as a dovetail saw or a **dozuki** saw, to do the cutting.*

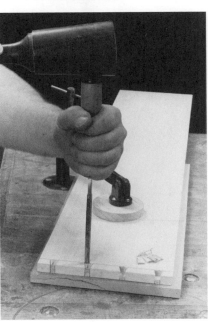

*4/Once you have cut the cheeks, remove the waste between the tails with a **very** sharp chisel. Remove each bit of waste in two steps. First, use the chisel as a cutting tool. Hold it vertically and place the edge on the baseline. Strike it with a mallet, cutting $1/16"–1/8"$ deep all along the line.*

5/Next, use the chisel as a wedge. Hold it horizontally and put the edge against the waste at the end of the board, $^1/_{16}" - ^1/_8"$ below the face. Strike it with a mallet, lifting a small amount of waste.

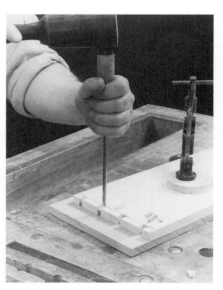

6/Repeat this procedure until you've cut halfway through the board. Then turn the board over and remove waste from the other side. Continue until you have removed all the waste between the tails.

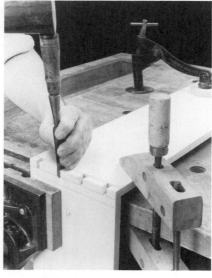

7/Scribe baselines on both sides of the adjoining board, then mark the pins. Use the completed tails as a template. (If you chose to make the pins first, you can use the completed pins to mark the tails.) Once again, shade the waste between the pins.

8/Saw the cheeks of the pins down to the baselines, cutting on the waste side of the marks. (This prevents you from removing too much stock.)

9/Remove the waste with a chisel, using the same cutting and wedging technique as before. Cut halfway through the board, turn it over, and remove the remaining waste.

10/Test the fit of the joint. Because you cut on the waste side of the marks when making both the tails and the pins, the fit is likely to be tight. If it's too tight, shave a little bit of stock from the pins with the chisel.

4 **Cut the shape of the sides.** Draw a full-size pattern of the sides shown in the *Side View,* and trace it onto the stock. Cut the shapes with a band saw or saber saw, then sand the sawed edges.

TRY THIS! To save time, stack one side on top of the other, with the dadoes facing each other. Tape the parts together, then cut and sand both parts at once.

5 **Drill the mounting holes.** The shelves are hung on the wall by nails or Molly anchors, which fit into ¼"-diameter, 1½"-deep mounting holes in the back of the shelves. Drill these holes near the top ends of the sides, at a 10° angle upward, as shown in the *Mounting Hole Detail.* This slight angle will keep the shelves from slipping off the nails or bolts.

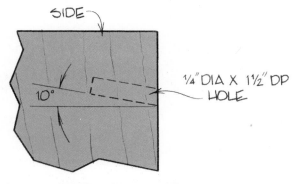

MOUNTING HOLE DETAIL

6 **Assemble the shelving unit.** Finish sand all the parts, then assemble them with nails and glue. The back edges of shelves must be flush with the back edges of the sides. Drive the nails through the sides, into the ends of the shelves. Set the heads and, if you wish, cover them with putty.

7 **Plane the front edges of the shelves.** Except for the bottom shelf, the front edges of the shelves should protrude about ⅛" beyond the front edges of the sides. Using a small hand plane, plane the front edges of these shelves until they're flush with the sides and at a matching angle.

8 **Apply a finish to the project.** With a rasp or file, round over the edges of the shelves and sides to make the piece look old and worn. Do any necessary touch-up sanding, then apply a finish to the completed project. After the finish dries, drive nails or install Molly anchors in a wall. Hang the shelves on these nails or bolts, slipping the mounting holes over them.

Bucket Bench

When America was first settled, every cabin had a "bucket bench" just outside the back door. This bench held two or three buckets of water for drinking, cooking, and washing. Empty buckets were quickly refilled so the cook always had fresh water.

The settlers built bucket benches in all shapes and sizes. Most had several shelves to help organize buckets and other items. On the bench shown, settlers probably kept the drinking water in the cupboard at the bottom. The cupboard doors prevented debris from settling in the drinking water. The shelf just above the cupboard held buckets of wash water at a comfortable height for washing the hands and face, dishes, and clothes. The small top shelf held soap, wash rags, dippers, and cups.

These simple (but indispensable) pieces quickly developed into more convenient forms. Craftsmen added work surfaces and splashboards, and when the piece moved inside, it became known as a dry sink. Later, indoor plumbing was added and the dry sink became the familiar kitchen sink. The old bucket bench began to serve other purposes. Today, they make useful display units or plant stands.

The bucket bench shown was built in the early nineteenth century by a Midwest furniture maker. As bucket benches go, it's fairly sophisticated. The design and construction — especially the doors — show a high degree of craftsmanship. ●

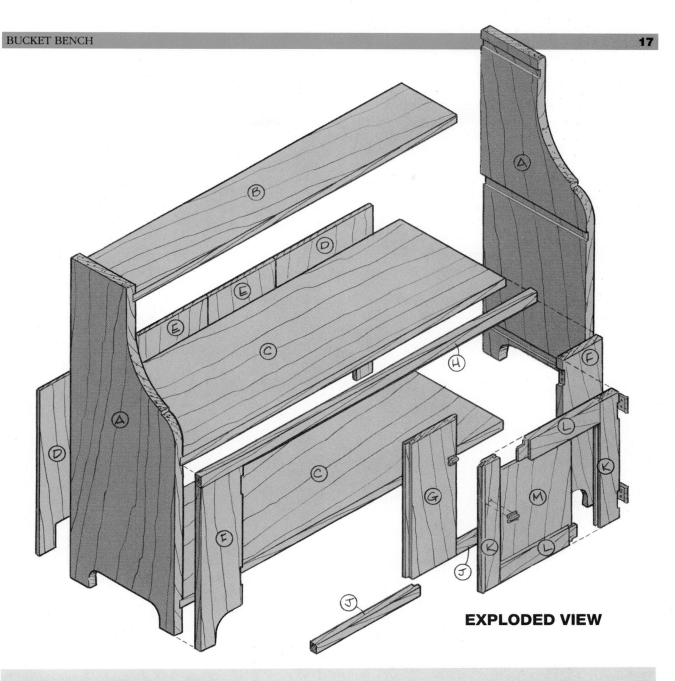

EXPLODED VIEW

Materials List

FINISHED DIMENSIONS

PARTS

A. Sides (2) $7/8'' \times 14^{3}/8'' \times 38^{3}/4''$

B. Top shelf $7/8'' \times 7^{1}/2'' \times 44^{3}/4''$

C. Middle/bottom shelves (2) $7/8'' \times 14^{3}/8'' \times 44^{3}/4''$

D. Outside backboards (2) $1/2'' \times$ (variable) $\times 20^{3}/4''$

E. Inside backboards (2–3) $1/2'' \times$ (variable) $\times 17^{5}/8''$

F. End stiles (2) $7/8'' \times 5^{1}/2'' \times 19^{7}/8''$

G. Middle stile $7/8'' \times 6^{3}/4'' \times 16^{3}/4''$

H. Top rail $7/8'' \times 1^{1}/4'' \times 46''$

J. Bottom rails (2) $7/8'' \times 1^{1}/4'' \times 14^{1}/2''$

K. Door stiles (4) $7/8'' \times 2^{1}/2'' \times 15^{3}/8''$

L. Door rails (4) $7/8'' \times 2^{1}/2'' \times 11^{3}/8''$

M. Door panels (2) $3/8'' \times 9^{7}/8'' \times 11^{1}/16''$

HARDWARE

$1^{3}/4'' \times 2''$ Butt hinges and mounting screws (2 pairs)

Door latches and mounting screws (2)

6d Square-cut nails (60–72)

1

***Select the stock and cut the parts to
size.*** To build this project, you'll need about
35 board feet of 4/4 (four-quarters) lumber. The bucket
bench shown is built from poplar, but country craftsmen also used white pine for utilitarian projects such
as this. However, you can use almost any cabinet-grade
wood. If you plan to paint the bench, you can even mix
various types of wood. To make a formal piece, use
cherry, walnut, or maple.

Plane approximately 6 board feet of lumber to ½″
thick. Resaw another 2 board feet in half, and plane the
pieces to ³⁄₈″ thick. Plane the remainder to ⅞″ thick.
(Depending on how your 4/4 stock is cut, it may be
hard to plane pieces ⅞″ thick — you may have to make
them slightly thinner. If so, adjust the other dimensions
as needed. Or, purchase 5/4 stock.) Cut all the parts to
the sizes shown, except the backboards and door parts.
You must fit these to the bench.

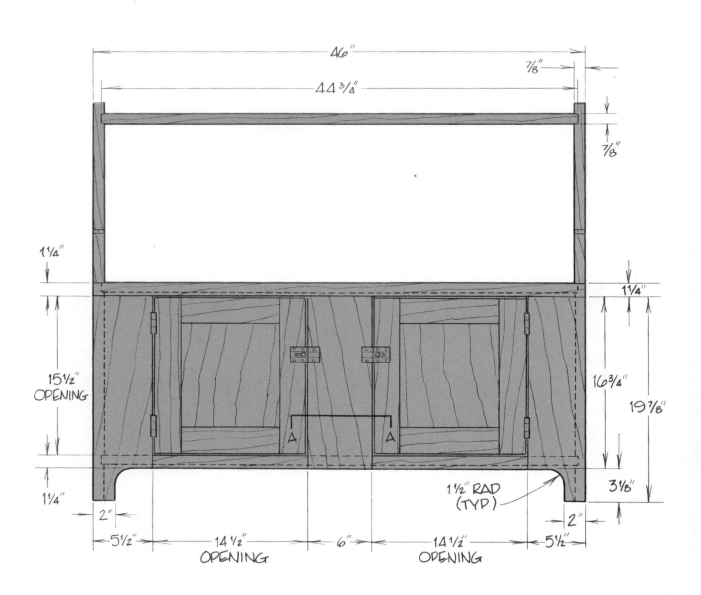

FRONT VIEW

2 Cut the joinery in the sides and middle shelf.

The case is assembled with simple dadoes and rabbets. Using a router or a dado cutter, cut the following joints:

- ■ ⁷⁄₈″-wide, ¼″-deep dadoes in the sides, as shown in the *Side Layout*
- ■ ½″-wide, ½″-deep blind rabbets in the back edges of the sides. Each rabbet should be 20¾″ long. Square the blind ends with a chisel.

- ■ ½″-wide, ½″-deep rabbet in the back edge of the middle shelf
- ■ ⅜″-wide, ½″-deep rabbets in both edges of the middle stile, as shown in *Section A*
- ■ ⅜″-wide, ⅜″-deep rabbets in the inside ends of the bottom rails

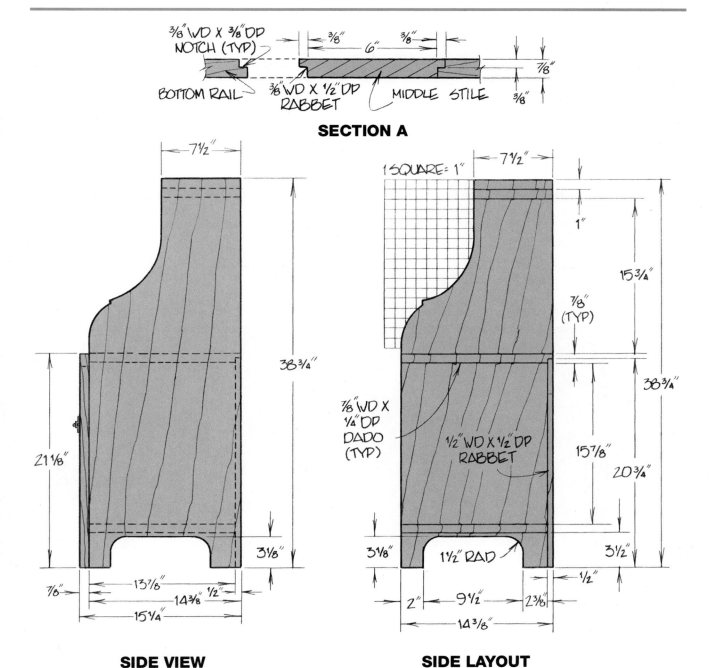

SECTION A

SIDE VIEW

SIDE LAYOUT

3 Cut the shape of the sides.

Cut the shape of the sides. Lay out the shape of the sides, as shown in the *Side Layout*. Cut the shapes with a band saw or saber saw, then sand the sawed edges.

TRY THIS! To save time, stack one side on top of the other, with the dadoes and rabbets facing each other. Tape the parts together, then cut and sand both at once.

4 Assemble the case.

Assemble the case. Finish sand all the parts, then assemble them with nails and glue, in this order:

- Attach the shelves to the sides.
- Attach the end stiles to the sides.
- Attach the top rail. Drive nails through the top rail into the top ends of the end stiles.

- Attach the middle stile. Again, drive nails down through the top rail into the top end of the stile.
- Attach the bottom rails.

When you drive square-cut nails, first drill $5/32''$-diameter pilot holes. This prevents the nails from splitting the wood. When you've assembled the case, set the heads of the nails. Cover them with putty, if you wish.

5 Attach the backboards to the case.

Attach the backboards to the case. Fit the backboards to the case, cutting and ripping them so they fit in the rabbets. These boards should be random widths, with about $1/16''$ between each board.

Using a band saw or saber saw, cut the legs in the outside backboards, as shown in the *Back Detail*. Attach the boards to the back with 4d nails, and set the heads.

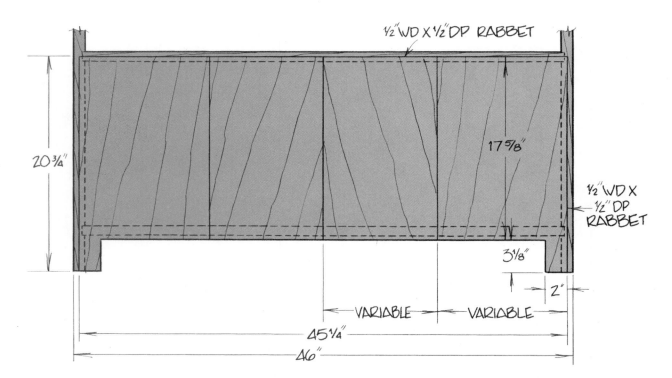

BACK DETAIL

6

Cut the parts for the door. Measure the door openings in the assembled case — they may have changed slightly from what's shown on the drawings. If so, adjust the dimensions of the door parts as necessary and cut them to size.

TRY THIS! **Many craftsmen prefer to make a door 1/16″–1/8″ oversize, then plane and sand the outside edges until they get a perfect fit.**

7

Cut the door joinery. Using a dado cutter or table-mounted router, cut ³/₈″-wide, ³/₈″-deep grooves in the inside edges of the door stiles and rails. Also cut ³/₈″-wide, 1″-long tenons on the ends of the rails. Using a band saw or a dovetail saw, notch these tenons as shown in the *Door Frame Assembly Detail*. These notches create a step or "haunch" in each tenon. (See Figure 1.)

To make the mortises, drill overlapping ³/₈″-diameter, 1″-deep holes in the stiles. Begin drilling ³/₈″ from the end of the stile. Make each series of holes 1³/₄″ long,

and center it in the grooved edge of the stile. (Measure the depth of the holes from the edge of the stile — not the bottom of the groove.) Square the corners and clean up the mortises with a small chisel. The haunched tenons must fit snugly in the mortises so the outside edges of the rails are flush with the ends of the stiles. (See Figure 2.)

Finally, cut ³/₈″-wide, ³/₈″-deep rabbets on the outside edges of the inside door stiles. These rabbets will overlap the rabbets on the middle stile.

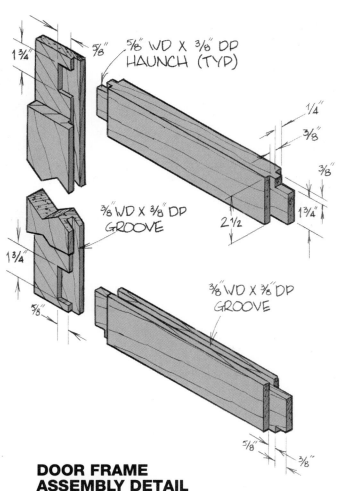

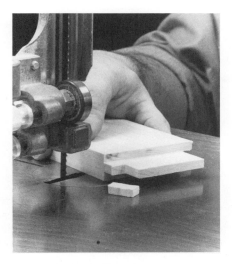

1/Using a band saw or a dovetail saw, cut a notch in the tenon, creating a step or "haunch." The haunch should be precisely as long as the grooves are deep.

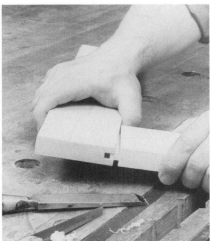

2/The haunched tenon should be snug in the mortise (but not too tight). When assembled, the outside edge of the rail must be flush with the end of the stile.

DOOR FRAME ASSEMBLY DETAIL

⅝″ WD X ³/₈″ DP HAUNCH (TYP)

³/₈″ WD X ³/₈″ DP GROOVE

³/₈″ WD X ³/₈″ DP GROOVE

8 **Cut beads in the stiles.** With a router or molder, cut a 5/16″ bead in the outside face of each inside door stile, as shown in the *Door Detail*. These beads — once called *cock beading* — were a popular decoration on eighteenth- and nineteenth-century door frames and drawer fronts.

DOOR DETAIL

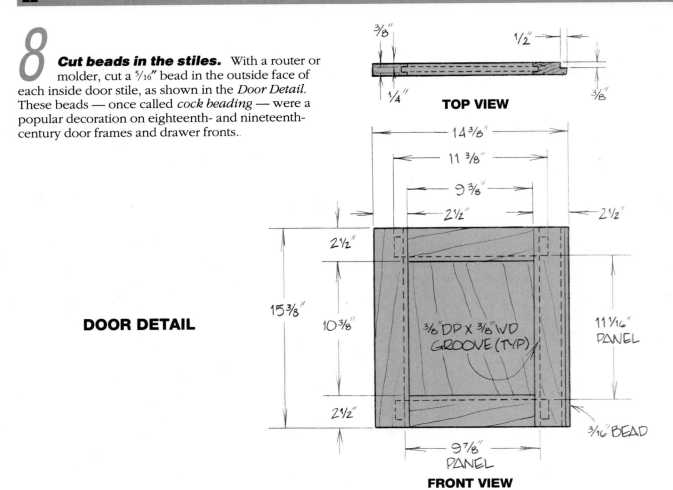

TOP VIEW

FRONT VIEW

9 **Assemble the door.** Finish sand the door parts, then glue the rails to the stiles. Place the door panel in the grooves as you assemble the frame. Do *not* glue it to the rails or stiles; let it float in the grooves.

TRY THIS! If you wish, drive pegs through the mortise-and-tenon joints to secure them.

10 **Hang the doors in the case.** Fit the doors in the case so there's about a 1/16″ gap all around them. Mortise the outside stiles and end stiles for hinges, then attach the door to the case. Afterward, attach the latches to the inside door stiles and middle stile.

11 **Finish the bucket bench.** Remove the doors from the bench, and the hinges and latches from the doors. With a rasp or file, round over the edges of the bench and doors to make the piece look old and worn. Do any necessary touch-up sanding, then apply a finish to the completed project. After the finish dries, replace the doors on the bench.

Pie-Safe Bookcase

Books were more precious in the eighteenth and nineteenth century than they are now. They were also more vulnerable to the elements. Moisture (or lack of it) might ruin leather bindings; insect larvae would eat glue and paper. Consequently, our ancestors protected their books better than we do. Whereas we think nothing of storing books on open shelves, they built closed bookcases to keep out the dust, moisture, and insects.

The earliest bookcases were adapted from many different forms of common storage furniture — cupboards, cabinets, dressers, and presses. At first, cabinetmakers changed the basic shapes very little; they simply substituted glazed doors for solid doors, and they enclosed open shelves. Both English and American craftsmen developed distinct designs for bookcases in the eighteenth century, but these were mostly for the rich. Ordinary folks continued to use modified cupboard and cabinet designs. It wasn't until much later that true bookcases became commonplace in country homes.

This nineteenth-century bookcase is one example of a country bookcase. It was built by a rural Ohio craftsman who, knowingly or unknowingly, patterned it after a traditional food press or *pie safe*. He substituted glass for the ventilated metal panels, and made the shelves adjustable. But the basic form remains the same as a pie safe.

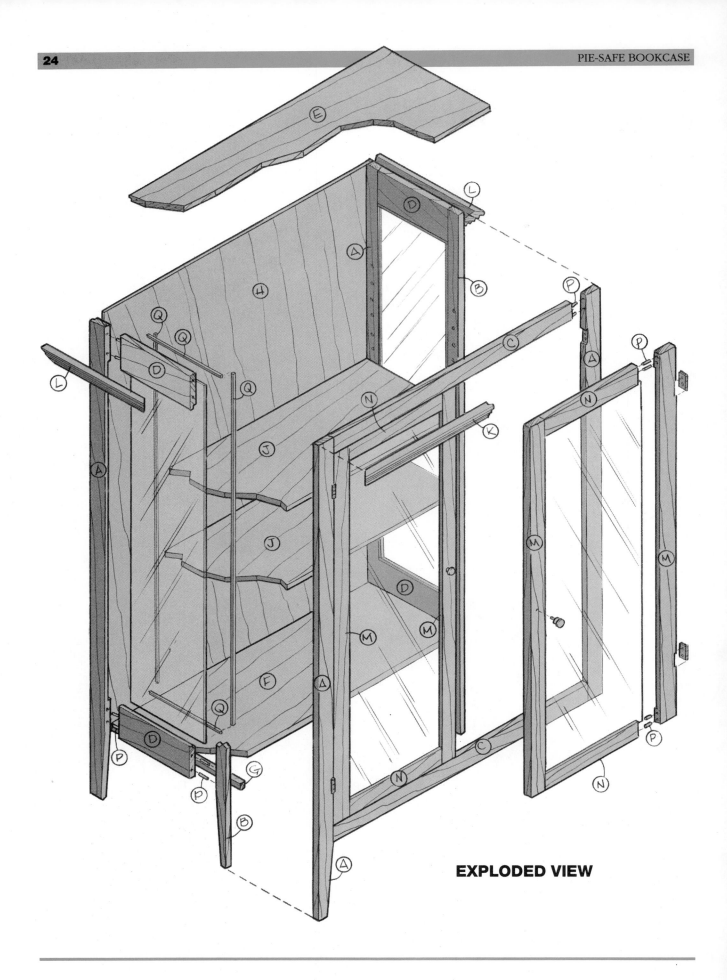

EXPLODED VIEW

Materials List

FINISHED DIMENSIONS

PARTS

A.	Wide legs (4)	$^3/_4$" x 2" x 58$^1/_4$"
B.	Narrow legs (2)	$^3/_4$" x 1$^1/_4$" x 58$^1/_4$"
C.	Front rails (2)	$^3/_4$" x 2" x 33"
D.	Side rails (4)	$^3/_4$" x 4" x 9$^1/_2$"
E.	Top	$^3/_4$" x 15$^1/_4$" x 40$^1/_2$"
F.	Bottom	$^3/_4$" x 12$^1/_4$" x 35$^1/_2$"
G.	Cleats (2)	$^3/_4$" x $^3/_4$" x 12$^3/_4$"
H.	Back	$^1/_2$" x 36$^1/_4$" x 48$^1/_2$"
J.	Adjustable shelves (2–4)	$^3/_4$" x 12$^1/_8$" x 35$^3/_8$"
K.	Front molding	$^3/_4$" x 2$^1/_8$" x 40"
L.	Side moldings (2)	$^3/_4$" x 2$^1/_8$" x 15"
M.	Door stiles (4)	$^3/_4$" x 2" x 45$^5/_8$"
N.	Door rails (4)	$^3/_4$" x 2" x 12$^3/_8$"
P.	Dowels (40)	$^3/_8$" dia. x 2"
Q.	Glazing strips (total)	$^1/_4$" x $^1/_4$" x 428"

HARDWARE

1$^1/_2$" x 3" Butt hinges (2 pairs)
Door pulls (2)
Bullet catches (4)
$^1/_8$" x 12$^{13}/_{16}$" x 42$^1/_{16}$" Glass panes (2)
$^1/_8$" x 9$^{15}/_{16}$" x 42$^3/_{16}$" Glass panes (2)
#8 x 1$^1/_4$" Flathead wood screws (40–48)
$^5/_8$" Wire brads (1 box)
2d Finishing nails (24–30)
Pin-style shelving supports (8–16)

---

1 Select the stock and cut the parts to size.

To build this project, you'll need about 35 board feet of 4/4 (four-quarters) lumber and a 4' x 8' sheet of cabinet-grade veneered plywood. The bookcase shown is made from cherry, but you can use any cabinet-grade hardwood. Most country furnituremakers preferred cherry, walnut, or figured maple for projects such as these. The plywood veneer should match or complement the hardwood.

After you've selected the lumber, plane 32 board feet of the stock to $^3/_4$" thick. Resaw the remainder in half, and plane it to $^1/_4$" thick. Glue up the wide boards needed for the top, bottom, and shelves. Cut all the parts to the sizes given in the Materials List *except* the door frame members, moldings, and glazing strips. Rip these to the proper width, but don't cut them to length — they must be fitted to the assembled cabinet.

Note: Choose the straightest, clearest stock you have to make the door rails and stiles. If these parts aren't perfectly straight, the doors may not fit the case properly.

---

2 Drill the shelving support holes.

The adjustable shelves are supported by pin-style supports. These supports fit in $^1/_4$"-diameter, $^3/_8$"-deep holes in the side legs, as shown in the *Narrow Side Leg Layout* and *Wide Side Leg Layout*. Carefully lay out and drill these holes so they are evenly spaced, 2" apart, on all four wide legs. (See Figure 1.)

1/To make sure the shelving support holes are spaced precisely the same on all four side legs, place the legs side by side on your workbench. Adjust them so the ends are even. Measure the location of the holes on one leg, then transfer these to the other three with a T-square, as shown.

3 Cut the rabbets that hold the back.
The back is rabbeted into the top and the side wide legs. Using a router and a straight bit, rout $\frac{1}{2}''$-wide, $\frac{3}{8}''$-deep rabbets in the back edges of these parts. The rabbets in the legs should be blind, as shown in the *Wide Side Leg Layout*. The rabbet in the top should be double-blind, as shown in the *Top Layout*. Square the blind ends with a chisel.

4 Cut tapers in the legs.
All the legs are tapered slightly, as shown in the *Front View* and *Side View*. Beginning $8\frac{1}{2}''$ from the bottom end, cut these tapers with a band saw or saber saw. Sand or joint the sawed edges.

5 Join the front and side frame members.
All the frames are joined with $\frac{3}{8}''$-diameter, 2''-long dowels, using two dowels in each joint. Mark the positions of the front and side rails on the adjoining stiles. Using a doweling jig to guide the drill, bore $\frac{3}{8}''$-diameter, 1''-deep dowel holes in the ends of the rails and the edges of the stiles.

Dry assemble the front and side frames to test the fit of the joints. When you're satisfied that all the joints fit properly, finish sand the frame members. Assemble the frames with dowels and glue. Let the glue dry, then sand the joints clean and flush.

> **TRY THIS!** If you wish, you can also join the frame members with wooden plates ("biscuits") or mortises and tenons. If you make mortise-and-tenon joints, you'll have to cut the rails longer than specified in the Materials List.

6 Rout the glass rabbets in the side frames.
The glass panels are rabbeted into the frames. Rout $\frac{1}{4}''$-wide, $\frac{3}{8}''$-deep rabbets in the *inside* edges of the side frames, then square the corners with a chisel.

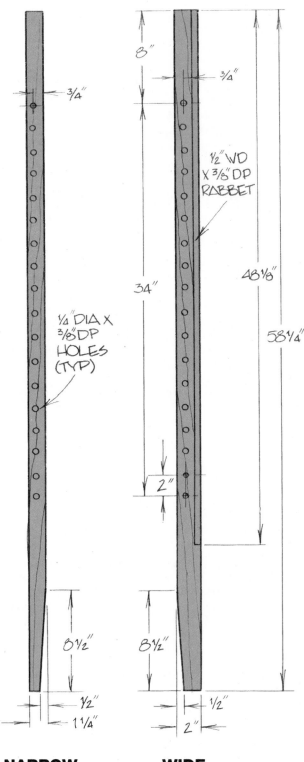

NARROW SIDE LEG LAYOUT

WIDE SIDE LEG LAYOUT

TOP LAYOUT

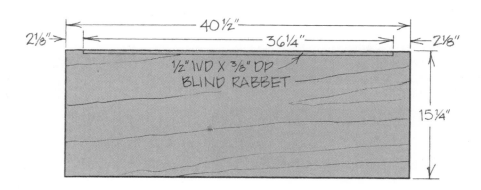

40½"
2⅛"
36¼"
2⅛"
½" WD X ⅜" DP
BLIND RABBET
15¼"

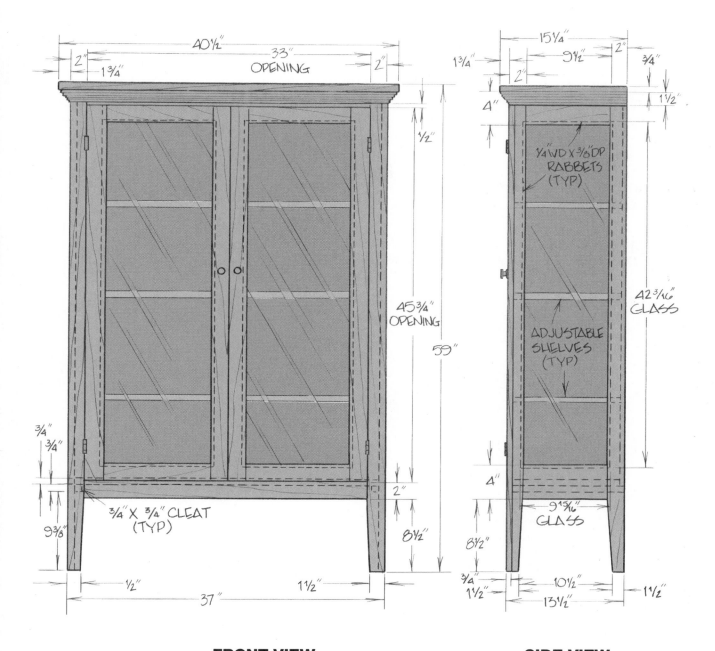

40½"
2"
1¾"
33"
OPENING
2"
½"
45¾"
OPENING
59"
¾"
¾"
¾" X ¾" CLEAT
(TYP)
9⅜"
2"
8½"
½"
1½"
37"

15¼"
1¾"
9½"
2"
¾"
2"
4"
1½"
¼" WD X ⅜" DP
RABBETS
(TYP)
42³⁄₁₆"
GLASS
ADJUSTABLE
SHELVES
(TYP)
4"
9¹⁵⁄₁₆"
GLASS
8½"
¾"
1½"
10½"
13½"
1½"

FRONT VIEW   **SIDE VIEW**

7 Assemble the case.

Assemble the case. Finish sand the top and bottom. Assemble the parts of the case in this order:

- Fasten the cleats to the side frame with glue and flathead wood screws. Countersink these screws so the heads are flush with the surface.
- Glue the side frame to the front frame. Before the glue dries, lay the bottom across the cleats.
- Fasten the top to the frames with screws. You can glue the top to the front frame, but do *not* glue it

to the side frame. Counterbore and countersink the screws, then cover their heads with wooden plugs. Sand the plugs flush with the surface.

- Glue the front edge of the bottom to the front frame, and fasten the bottom to the cleats with screws. Countersink the screws. Do *not* glue the bottom to the cleats.

Note: Do *not* attach the back yet.

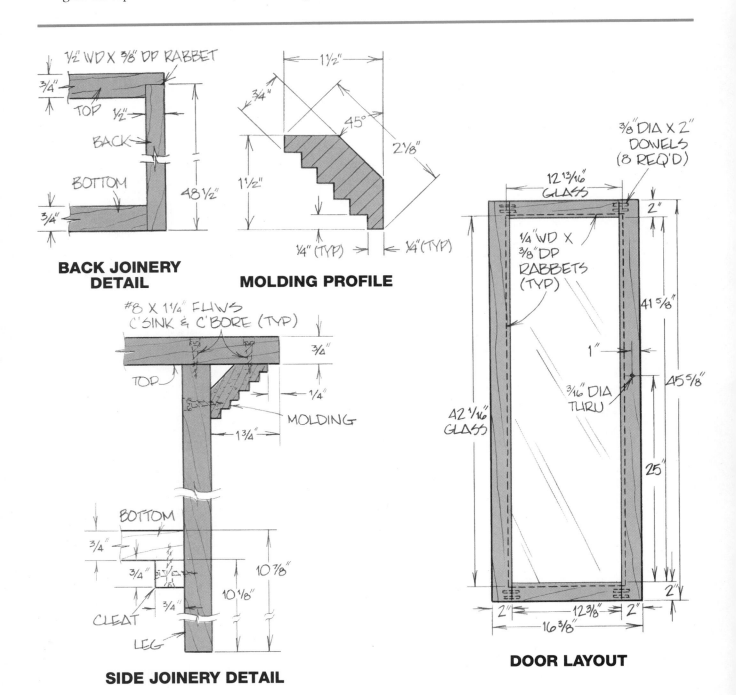

BACK JOINERY DETAIL

MOLDING PROFILE

SIDE JOINERY DETAIL

DOOR LAYOUT

8 Cut the molding profile.

The molding around the top of the case is "step" molding. To make this, mount a dado cutter in your table saw, stacked to cut a $\frac{1}{4}''$-wide kerf. Tilt the accessory to 45°. Using the fence as a guide, cut a single $\frac{1}{4}''$-wide, $\frac{1}{4}''$-deep step. Move the fence $\frac{5}{16}''$ and cut a second step. Repeat until you have cut all the steps. (See Figure 2.) Replace the dado cutter with a saw blade, and bevel the edges of the stock at 45°.

> **TRY THIS!** You can also cut these steps with a table-mounted router and a large V-groove bit. Or, you can substitute a different shape for the molding — cove, crown, bed, or one of your own devising.

2/Cut the step molding with a dado cutter, tilted to 45°. You must use an ordinary stacked dado accessory. Don't try to use a wobble dado blade for this operation.

9 Attach the molding to the case.

Carefully fit the molding to the case, compound-mitering the adjoining ends at 45°. (See Figure 3.) Attach the molding to the case and top with screws, as shown in the *Side Joinery Detail*. Counterbore and countersink the screws, then cover their heads with plugs. Sand the plugs flush with the surface.

3/Make a simple L-shaped jig as shown to help cut the molding. Attach this jig to the miter gauge, and place the molding in it. The jig will hold the molding so you can easily cut the compound miters.

10 Attach the back to the case.

Finish sand the back. Fasten it to the top, bottom, and side legs with finishing nails. Set the heads of the nails.

You may glue the back in place if you wish, but most furnituremakers prefer not to. This makes it easy to replace the plywood, should it ever delaminate.

11 Assemble the door frames.

Carefully measure the door opening in the case. It may have changed slightly from the dimensions shown on the drawings. (This is normal when assembling large case pieces.) If so, adjust the measurements of the door rails and stiles so the assembled doors will be approximately $\frac{1}{16}''$ *smaller* than the opening, all the way around. Cut the parts to length.

Finish sand the rails and stiles, then assemble and rabbet the door frames in the same manner as the side and front frames. Join the rails and stiles with dowels, and sand the joints clean and flush. Then rout rabbets in the inside edges to hold the glass panels.

> **TRY THIS!** You may wish to cut the door frame members $\frac{1}{8}''$ long. The assembled door frames will be slightly oversize, but you can fit them precisely to the opening by planing or sanding the edge.

12

Mount the doors in the case. Mortise the outside door stiles and front legs for butt hinges. Mount the doors in the case, and mount pulls on the doors. Bore the top and bottom ends of the inside door stiles, and mount bullet catches in the holes. (The size and depth of these holes will depend on the size of the catches.) Mortise the front frame rails for the catch plates, and mount the plates. (See Figure 4.)

4/A bullet catch consists of a bullet-shaped cylinder and a plate. Mount the cylinder in a hole in the door frame, and mortise the catch into the front frame.

13

Cut the glazing strips. Cut the glazing strips to fit inside the rabbets in the door and side frames. Miter the adjoining ends at 45°.

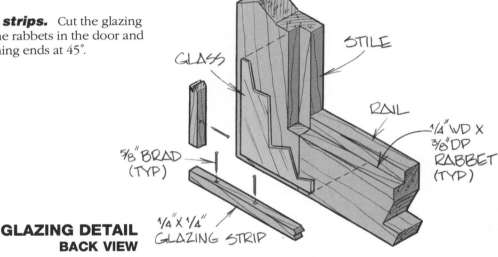

GLASS

STILE

RAIL

¼" WD X ⅜" DP RABBET (TYP)

⅝" BRAD (TYP)

GLAZING DETAIL
BACK VIEW

¼" X ¼" GLAZING STRIP

14

Apply a finish. Remove the doors from the case, and all the hardware from the doors. Also remove the catch plates from the case. Finish sand the adjustable shelves, and do any necessary touch-up sanding to the case and door frames. Apply a finish to all sides (inside, outside, top, and bottom) of the bookcase, door frames, and shelves. Apply a finish to the glazing strips, also.

15

Install the glass. Replace the hardware and doors on the case. Place the glass panes in their frames, then fasten them in place with glazing strips. Drive wire brads through each strip and into the frame member. Set the heads of the brads. Do *not* glue the glazing strips in place, in case you need to remove them someday.

Southwest "Repisa"

Although most of our furniture designs are derived from European traditions, European immigrants did not make the first furniture in this country. It was made by native Americans. In 1521, when the Spanish conquered the area we now call Arizona and New Mexico, they found that the Pueblo Indians and their neighbors had a rich woodworking tradition dating back centuries.

The Spanish enslaved the Indians and taught them to make furniture based on traditional Old World designs. Among them was this two-step shelving unit, called a *repisa*. The Indians were often forced to build this immigrant furniture, but they modified the forms and added their own decorative features. For example, the rectangular shapes on this *repisa* are Pueblo "cloud steps," a common design element among many Indians in the southwest United States and Mexico.

The Indian carpenters eventually developed unique furniture designs, distinct from both Spanish and pre-Columbian Indian furniture. They made these pieces for over two centuries in and around the Spanish mission towns. We now call them Southwest country furniture. ●

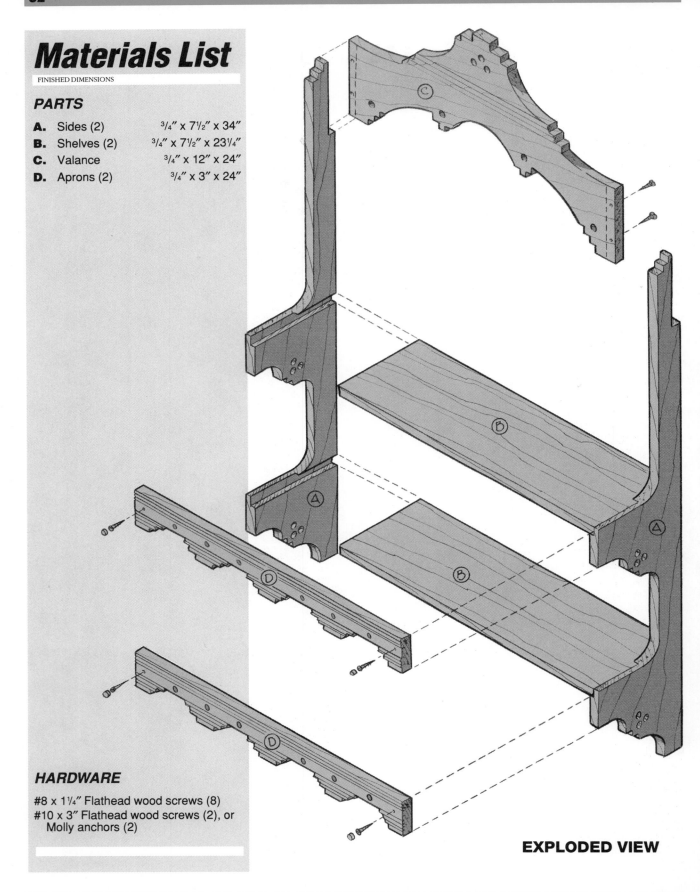

Materials List

FINISHED DIMENSIONS

PARTS

A. Sides (2) $3/4'' \times 7\frac{1}{2}'' \times 34''$
B. Shelves (2) $3/4'' \times 7\frac{1}{2}'' \times 23\frac{1}{4}''$
C. Valance $3/4'' \times 12'' \times 24''$
D. Aprons (2) $3/4'' \times 3'' \times 24''$

HARDWARE

#8 x 1¼" Flathead wood screws (8)
#10 x 3" Flathead wood screws (2), or
   Molly anchors (2)

EXPLODED VIEW

1 **Select the stock and cut the parts to size.** To make this project, you'll need about 14 board feet of 4/4 (four-quarters) lumber. Southwest Indian craftsmen worked almost exclusively with pon-derosa pine. However, you can use almost any cabinet-grade softwood. Avoid redwood and red cedar because they split too easily. After you've selected the stock, cut the parts to the sizes given in the Materials List.

2 **Cut the beads in the valance and aprons.** With a table-mounted router or a molder, cut ⁵⁄₁₆″ beads in the valance and apron stock, as shown in the *Front View* and *Apron Profile*. Make 3 beads in the valance, and 6 in each apron. If you cut these shapes with a router, use a point-cut quarter-round bit and make the shapes in several passes. If you're using a molder, use three-bead knives, and cut the shapes in one pass. (See Figures 1 and 2.)

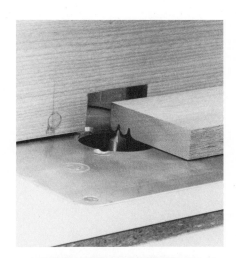

1/There are two ways to cut the beads in the valance and aprons. You can use a table-mounted router and a point-cut quarter-round bit as shown. Guide the stock with a fence. Make the beads in several passes, moving the fence slightly with each pass.

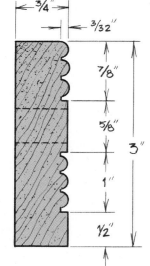

APRON PROFILE

3/4″
3/32″
7/8″
5/8″
3″
1″
1/2″

2/You can also use a molder and a set of three-bead knives. As the name implies, these knives will cut three beads in one pass.

3 **Cut the dadoes in the sides.** The shelves are dadoed into the sides, as shown in the *Front View*. Using a router or a dado cutter, cut 3/4″-wide, 3/8″-deep dadoes in the sides.

4 **Cut and drill the shapes of the sides, aprons, and valance.** Enlarge the *Side Pattern, Apron Pattern,* and *Valance Pattern*. Trace these on the stock, then cut the shapes with a band saw or saber saw. Sand the sawed edges.

Drill 1/2″-diameter holes through the sides, aprons, and valance, where shown on the patterns. These holes are decorative and serve no practical purpose. You may omit them, if you prefer.

5 Assemble the shelves.

Assemble the shelves. Finish sand all the parts, then assemble them in this order:

■ Glue the shelves in the side dadoes.

■ Glue the valance to the sides. Reinforce the glue joint with flathead wood screws. Countersink the screws so the heads are flush with the surface of the wood.

■ Glue the aprons to the shelves and sides. Reinforce these joints with flathead wood screws. Use the screws only at the ends of the aprons, where the aprons join the sides. Counterbore and countersink the screws, then cover the heads with wooden plugs. Sand the plugs flush with the surface.

After the glue dries, sand all joints clean and flush.

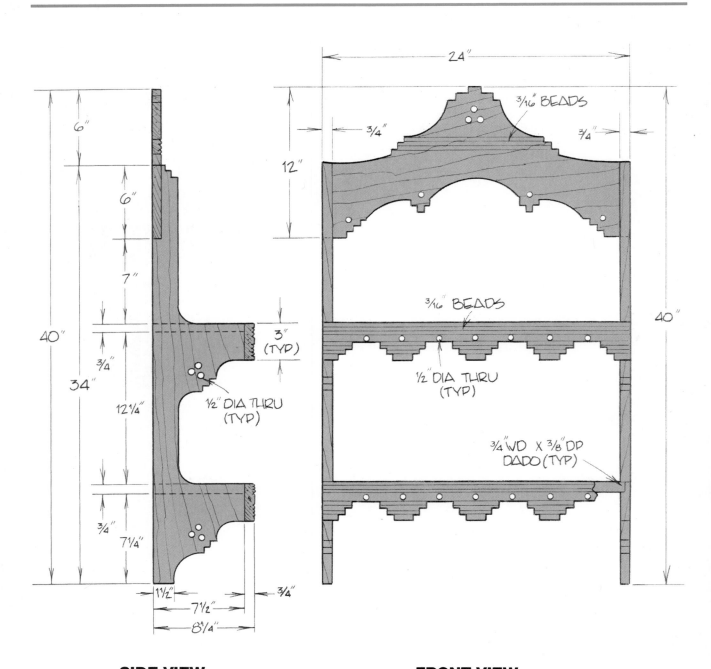

SIDE VIEW   **FRONT VIEW**

6 ***Finish and mount the repisa.*** Do any necessary touch-up sanding, then apply a finish to the project. When the finish dries, mount the *repisa* on a wall.

To attach the *repisa* to the studs in the wall, use flathead wood screws. Drive the screws through the valance and into the wall. Counterbore and countersink the screws, then cover the heads with plugs. If you can't attach the *repisa* to studs, install Molly anchors in the wall. Drive the Molly bolts through the valance and into the anchors.

TRY THIS! Instead of attaching the *repisa* to the wall, you may also install metal hangers or rout keyhole slots in the back of the valance. Hang the project as you would a large picture.

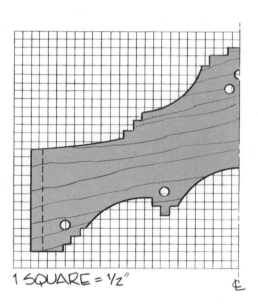

1 SQUARE = ½"

VALANCE PATTERN

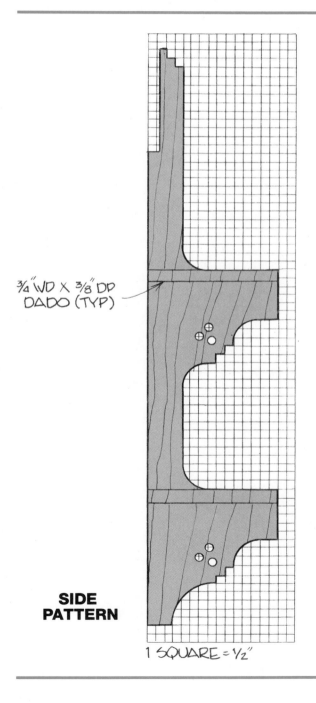

¾" WD X ⅜" DP DADO (TYP)

SIDE PATTERN

1 SQUARE = ½"

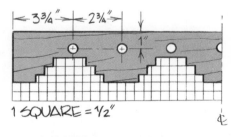

1 SQUARE = ½"

APRON PATTERN
WITHOUT BEADING

Clock Shelf

The earliest — and simplest — country storage devices were hanging shelves. English peasants have hung shelves in their homes since medieval times, using them to hold or display cups, dishes, and other small items. Each of these shelves consisted of a single board and two or more brackets to support it — what we call a bracket shelf. The basic design of these shelves hasn't changed in a thousand years.

The bracket shelf shown is similar to many of the clock shelves that adorned country homes in the early nineteenth century. At the beginning of the Industrial Revolution, American clockmakers invented mantle clocks, miniaturized versions of grandfather clocks. Because they cost so much less than larger clocks, mantle clocks became popular among folks of modest means, who previously couldn't afford a timepiece. However, not everyone had a mantle to put them on. So country cabinetmakers made decorative bracket shelves such as this to hold the clocks, and hung them on their walls.

Materials List

FINISHED DIMENSIONS

PARTS

A. Shelf $^3/_4$" x $8^3/_4$" x 26"
B. Brackets (2) $^3/_4$" x $5^3/_8$" x $6^3/_8$"
C. Wall plates (2) $^3/_4$" x 3" x $6^3/_8$"

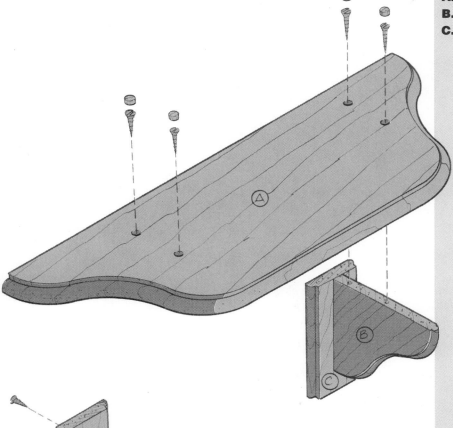

EXPLODED VIEW

HARDWARE

#8 x $1^1/_4$" Flathead wood screws (8)
#10 x 4" Roundhead wood screws and
   washers (2), or Molly anchors (2)

1 Select the stock and cut the parts to size. To build this project, you need about 3 board feet of 4/4 (four-quarters) lumber. Since you can use any kind of cabinet-grade wood, consider using scrap wood, particularly if you have been saving some special pieces. After selecting the lumber, cut all the parts to the sizes given in the Materials List.

2 Cut the shapes of the shelf and brackets. Enlarge the shelf and bracket patterns, as shown in the *Top View* and *Side View*. Trace these on the stock, then cut the shapes with a band saw or saber saw. Sand the sawed edges.

3 Shape the edges of the parts. Using a router or shaper, cut beads and steps in the front and side edges of all the parts. Use a ½″ quarter-round bit or cutter to shape the shelf and plates, and a ¼″ quarter-round bit or cutter to shape the brackets. Sand the shaped edges smooth.

4 Assemble the plates and brackets. Finish sand all the parts — shelf, plates, and brackets. Glue the brackets to the plates. Reinforce the glue bond with flathead wood screws. Countersink the screws, so the heads are flush with the surface of the wood.

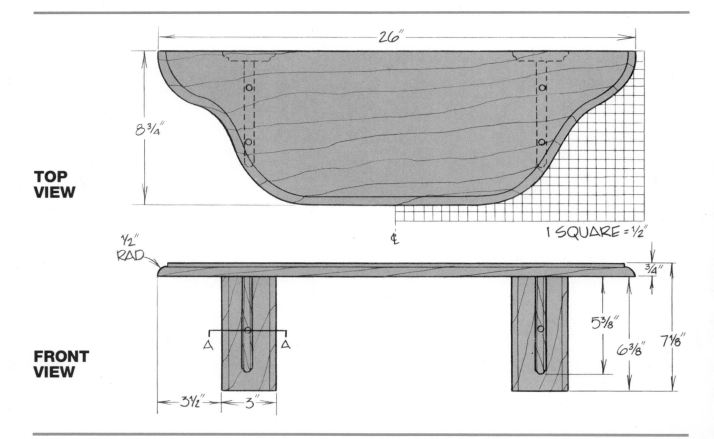

TOP VIEW

FRONT VIEW

5

Drill the mounting holes.   Place a bracket
assembly on a drill press, with the plate flat on
the worktable. Drill a $7/16''$-diameter counterbore part-
way through the bracket, as shown in *Section A*. Then
drill a $3/16''$-diameter pilot hole through the counterbore
and the rest of the way through the bracket and plate.
(See Figure 1.) Repeat for the other bracket assembly.

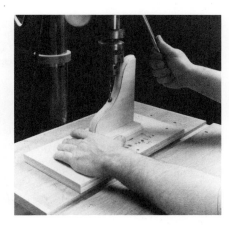

1/Drill the counter-
bore first, then the
pilot hole. When
making deep holes
such as these,
retract the drill now
and then to clear
the wood chips.
This will prevent
the bit from wander-
ing or overheating.

6

Attach the shelf to the brackets.   Glue
the shelf to the brackets, then reinforce the joints
with flathead wood screws. Counterbore and countersink
these screws, and cover the heads with wooden plugs.
Sand the plugs flush with the surface of the wood.

7

Finish and mount the shelf.   Do any necessary touch-up sanding, then apply a finish to the
project. When the finish dries, mount the shelf on a wall.
   To attach the shelf to the frame studs in the wall, use
roundhead wood screws and washers. Put the washers
on the screws, then insert the screws in the bracket
counterbores. Drive the screws through the brackets
and plates, and into the wall. If you can't attach one
or both brackets to studs, install a Molly anchor in the
wall where you want to secure each bracket. Pass the
Molly bolt through the counterbore, and tighten it in
the anchor.
   Note: In most homes, studs are either $16''$ or $24''$
apart, on center. As designed, the brackets on this shelf
are exactly $16''$ apart, for mounting on a wall in which
the studs are also $16''$ apart. If the studs in your house
are $24''$ apart, you may wish to lengthen the shelf.

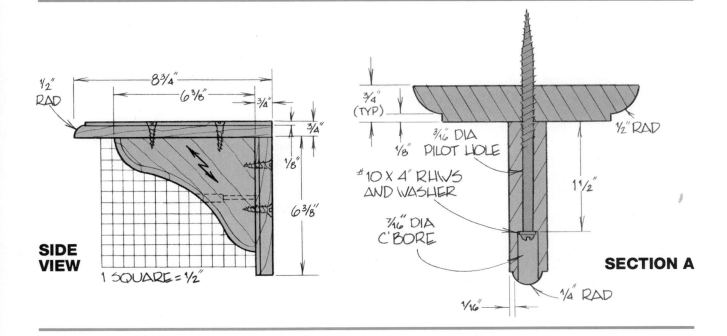

SIDE
VIEW

1 SQUARE = $1/2''$

SECTION A

Aging Country Furniture

To make accurate reproductions of country furniture, you must make the new project look old. This sounds simpler than it really is. For a piece to seem timeworn, you must pay careful attention to the details — materials, construction, and finishes. The piece must be built and finished in the same manner that an eighteenth- or nineteenth-century country cabinetmaker may have done. Then you must simulate over a hundred years of use and abuse.

Selecting Materials

To make your project look old, start by choosing the materials an old-time cabinetmaker would have chosen. You can use almost any cabinet-grade hardwood or softwood. However, avoid processed wood products such as plywood. Plywood is recommended in some of the chapters, but usually only for extremely wide parts (backs of cabinets, for example) and parts you can't see in the assembled project. This simplifies construction and adds strength without detracting from the old country appearance. But if historical accuracy is important to you, use solid wood instead.

You should also select the appropriate hardware. Country craftsmen didn't have the enormous selection we have today. Most of their hardware was made by a local blacksmith from iron. Brass was expensive and had to be shipped from large cities. It was used sparingly, if at all, and mostly on important, formal pieces. They didn't have roundhead screws; all old-time screws had flat heads. Nor did they have round nails, just square ones. (See Figure A.)

Here are good sources for hand-forged or period hardware:

Ball and Ball
463 W. Lincoln Highway
Exton, PA 19341

The Wise Company
6503 St. Claude Avenue
Arabi, LA 70032

Tremont Nail Company
8 Elm Street
P.O. Box 111
Wareham, MA 02571

To remove the shine from brasses and make them look older, soak them in paint stripper for 20–30 minutes. This removes the protective lacquer coat. Rinse off the stripper with alcohol. The brasses will begin to tarnish naturally in a few days.

To make store-bought iron hardware look older, soak it in a 40-percent solution of nitric acid (2 parts acid, 3 parts distilled water) for 5–10 minutes. This strips away the rust-resistant zinc chromate plating. Rinse the hardware in distilled water, blot it dry (but don't dry it completely), and immediately dip it in gun bluing solution. Let it sit for 3–5 minutes, blot it dry again, and let it sit overnight. In the morning, most of the surfaces will be black, and there will be a slight tinge of rust in the crevices. (See Figure B.)

Warning: When using nitric acid, always work outdoors and avoid breathing the fumes. Wear a long-sleeve shirt, pants, rubber gloves, and a full face shield. And use a large glass container.

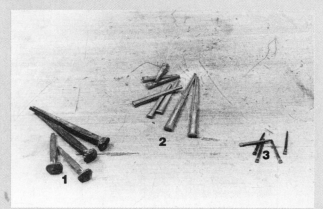

A/Country craftsmen used square-shanked, hand-forged nails like these. **Rose-head nails** (1) were common until 1800, when new nail-making machinery made **plancher nails** (2) less expensive and more available. **Headless brads** (3) were used throughout the eighteenth and nineteenth centuries.

B/Treat store-bought hardware — hinges, catches, screws, and so on — with nitric acid and gun bluing to make it appear old and rusty.

Preparing the Surface

If you visit a museum of old tools, you'll notice several important differences between your tools and those of country craftsmen. The most obvious, of course, is that you have many power tools, whereas they worked mostly by hand. However, there is a more subtle — and more important — difference. Your power tools cut the wood with a *rotary* motion. Except for a few braces, bits, and augers, the country craftsman's tools all cut in a *straight line,* leaving a distinctly different surface on wood.

To make your project look as if it could have been made with hand tools, you must remove all evidence of machining. Carefully sand or scrape away the wavelike mill marks left by planers, jointers, routers, shapers, molders, and similar tools. If a rough-sawed surface will show on your project (the underside of a drawer, for example), resaw the board with a band saw — one of the few power tools that cuts in a straight line. Vary the feed rate as you cut so the saw marks are uneven.

Aging a Finish

The most important step in making a project look old is to age the finish, because it shows the most wear and tear. Apply the finish as you normally would, then use these techniques to make it look timeworn.

Using a file or sandpaper, round over or "break" the hard corners and edges, especially those that would have gotten the most use — edges of doors, corners of table tops, areas around pulls and latches. Cut through the finish and into the raw wood in these areas. (See Figure C.) Some contemporary country furnituremakers repeat this step several times, building up several layers of worn finishes to create a "finish history." This really happened to many historical pieces! Typically, they were painted with a brightly colored milk paint, then covered with a dark lacquer during Victorian times, then a light-colored enamel in the twentieth century.

After applying and aging the finish, distress the surface — create tiny dents and dings that would have been made over time. (Some craftsmen do this before applying the finish, but this is a mistake. It doesn't happen that way in real life.) You can make your own distressing tool by wiring 20–30 old keys to a handle. (See Figure D.) *Lightly* beat the surface with the keys. Be careful; it's very easy to overdo this step! Don't make too many dents or use heavy tools such as chains or hammers. The surface should look worn — not like it has been through a war.

Finally, add some simulated dirt and grime. Dilute a dark stain or glaze to the point that it will tint the finish slightly darker, but not completely cover it. (Experiment with different mixtures on a scrap board until you achieve the effect you want.) Apply this mixture to the project, wiping it over the entire surface. The diluted stain will soak into the areas of raw wood, turning them darker. It will also stay in the dents and crevices, looking like years of accumulated dirt. Let the stain dry, then seal the surface with a clear finish — lacquer, shellac, or varnish.

C/To make the finish look worn, sand the areas that would have seen the most use, exposing the raw wood beneath them. Also, round over the corners and sharp edges.

D/Make a distressing tool from a bunch of old keys and **lightly** beat the surface of the project with them. Make small dents and dings, but don't overdo it. The surface wear must be believable.

Open Highboy

Not all country furniture has a historical precedent. Now and then, you run across a unique piece that a craftsman created out of whole cloth. This open highboy is one example. At first, you might think it is a countrified version of a Victorian display stand or *etagere*. However, this piece was built in the early 1800s, and display stands didn't become common until much later. The craftsman anticipated the new form by almost a century!

At the time this piece was built, it was common practice to put enclosed cupboards and chests on stands. (The classic highboy had developed from this design a century earlier.) It was also customary to put open shelves on an enclosed base to make a dish dresser or hutch. But open shelves on a highboy-type stand were very rare. The country cabinetmaker who built this piece either worked from an original design given to him by a client, or developed his own design. While it may be a historical oddity, it is nonetheless a charming one. ✦

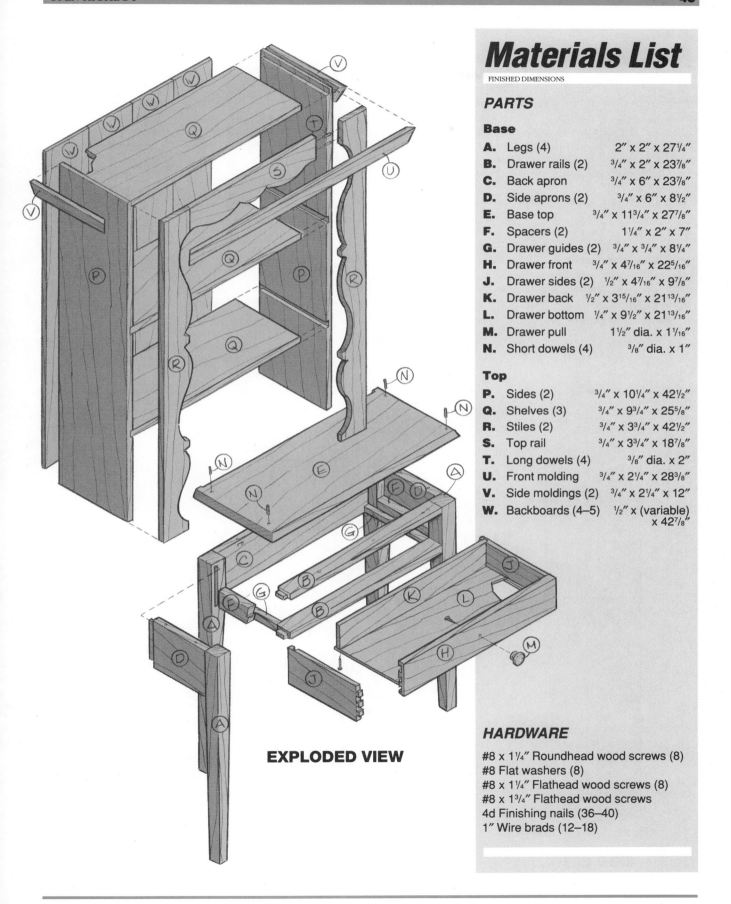

EXPLODED VIEW

Materials List

FINISHED DIMENSIONS

PARTS

Base

A.	Legs (4)	2" x 2" x 27¼"
B.	Drawer rails (2)	¾" x 2" x 23⅞"
C.	Back apron	¾" x 6" x 23⅞"
D.	Side aprons (2)	¾" x 6" x 8½"
E.	Base top	¾" x 11¾" x 27⅞"
F.	Spacers (2)	1¼" x 2" x 7"
G.	Drawer guides (2)	¾" x ¾" x 8¼"
H.	Drawer front	¾" x 4⁷⁄₁₆" x 22⁵⁄₁₆"
J.	Drawer sides (2)	½" x 4⁷⁄₁₆" x 9⅞"
K.	Drawer back	½" x 3¹⁵⁄₁₆" x 21¹³⁄₁₆"
L.	Drawer bottom	¼" x 9½" x 21¹³⁄₁₆"
M.	Drawer pull	1½" dia. x 1¹⁄₁₆"
N.	Short dowels (4)	⅜" dia. x 1"

Top

P.	Sides (2)	¾" x 10¼" x 42½"
Q.	Shelves (3)	¾" x 9¾" x 25⅝"
R.	Stiles (2)	¾" x 3¾" x 42½"
S.	Top rail	¾" x 3¾" x 18⅞"
T.	Long dowels (4)	⅜" dia. x 2"
U.	Front molding	¾" x 2¼" x 28⅜"
V.	Side moldings (2)	¾" x 2¼" x 12"
W.	Backboards (4–5)	½" x (variable) x 42⅞"

HARDWARE

#8 x 1¼" Roundhead wood screws (8)
#8 Flat washers (8)
#8 x 1¼" Flathead wood screws (8)
#8 x 1¾" Flathead wood screws
4d Finishing nails (36–40)
1" Wire brads (12–18)

1

Select the stock and cut the parts to size.   To make this project, you need about 36 board feet of 4/4 (four-quarters) lumber, 5 board feet of 10/4 (ten-quarters) stock, and a scrap of ¼" cabinet-grade plywood. The highboy shown is made from poplar. However, you can use any cabinet-grade wood.

Plane the 10/4 stock to 2" thick, and cut it into 2" x 2" squares to make the legs. Also, cut a turning square for the drawer pull. Plane the leftover 2"-thick stock to 1¼"

thick to make the spacers. Thickness 10 board feet of the 4/4 stock to ½" for the backboards, drawer sides, and drawer back. Plane the remaining 4/4 stock to ¾".

Cut the parts to the sizes shown in the Materials List, except the drawer parts, backboard, and moldings. You must fit these to the assembled project. Bevel both ends and one edge of the base top at 30°, as shown in the *Base Top Layout*.

2

Cut the joinery.   Lay out the joinery on the sides, base top, legs, aprons, and base rails. Rout or cut the joints needed to assemble the project:

- ¾"-wide, ⅜"-deep dadoes in the sides to hold the middle and bottom shelves, as shown in the *Side Layout*
- ¾"-wide, ⅜"-deep rabbet in the sides to hold the top shelf

- ½"-wide, ⅜"-deep rabbets in the sides to hold the backboards
- ½"-wide, ⅜"-deep double-blind rabbet in the base top to hold the backboards, as shown in the *Base Top Layout*
- ⅜"-wide, ¾"-deep, 4¾"-long mortises in all the legs to hold the side and back aprons, as shown in the *Left Front Leg Layout* and *Right Back Leg Layout*

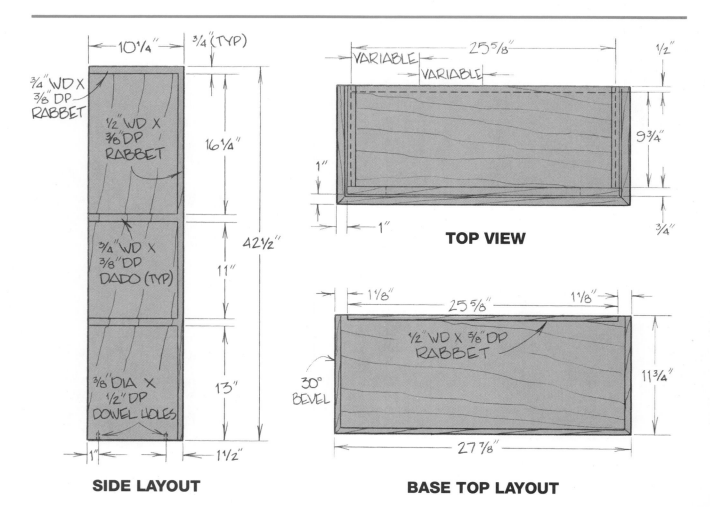

SIDE LAYOUT   **BASE TOP LAYOUT**

- ³/₈"-wide, 1¹/₄"-long, ³/₄"-deep mortises in the front legs to hold the rails
- A ³/₈"-thick, ³/₄"-long tenon on the ends of the aprons and base rails to join the legs

Using a chisel, square the blind ends of the base top rabbet and leg mortises. Then, with a band saw or dovetail saw, trim the width of the tenons on the rails and aprons, fitting them to the leg mortises.

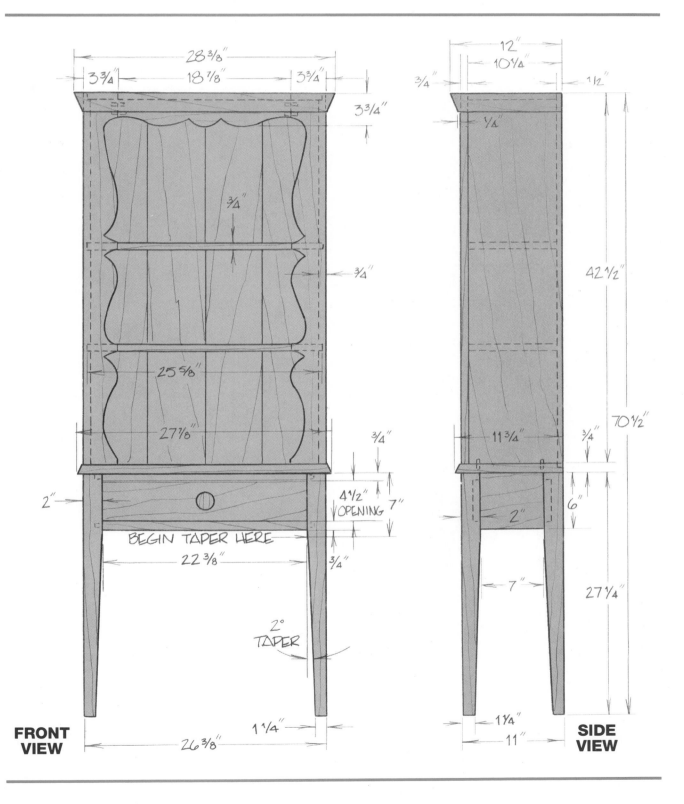

FRONT VIEW

SIDE VIEW

3

Taper the legs. As shown in the *Front View,* each leg tapers from 2″ to 1¼″ on the *two inside surfaces only.* Beginning 7″ from the top end, cut the tapers with a tapering jig.

Note: Do *not* taper the legs until after you have mortised them. It's almost impossible to cut accurate joints after the legs have been tapered.

TRY THIS! You can make your own tapering jig from a scrap of plywood, as shown in the illustration. This jig is designed to taper a board ¾″ over a cut 20¼″ long — the same taper needed for the highboy legs. Cut the tapering jig with a band saw or saber saw.

TAPERING JIG

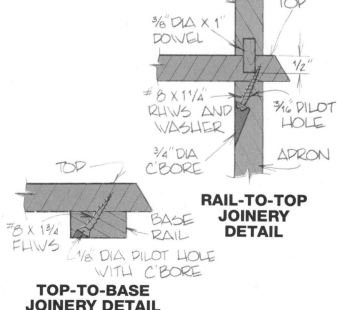

4

Drill the screw pockets and pilot holes. The base top is secured to the aprons and base rail with screws. Drill screw pockets for the screws that hold the base top to the aprons, as shown in the *Top-to-Base Joinery Detail.* (See Figure 1.) Make two screw pockets in each side apron, and three in the back apron. The spacing of the pockets isn't critical, but it should be fairly even.

For those screws that hold the base top to the rails, drill angled pilot holes. These are shown in the *Rail-to-Top Joinery Detail.* The angle makes it easier to drive the screws through the rails, after they are attached to the legs.

1/To make a screw pocket, tilt the work table of a drill press to 15°, and clamp a fence on it to help support the stock. Drill the counterbore or "pocket" first, stopping about ½″ before you reach the edge of the board. Then drill the pilot hole, centering it in the counterbore. The pilot hole should exit the board in the center of the edge.

SIDE

TOP

⅜″ DIA X 1″ DOWEL

½″

#8 X 1¼″ RHWS AND WASHER

³⁄₁₆″ PILOT HOLE

¾″ DIA C'BORE

APRON

RAIL-TO-TOP JOINERY DETAIL

TOP

BASE RAIL

#8 X 1¾″ FHWS

⅛″ DIA PILOT HOLE WITH C'BORE

TOP-TO-BASE JOINERY DETAIL

5

Drill the dowel holes. The top assembly mounts to the base with four dowels, which rest in holes in the sides. Using a doweling jig to guide the drill, bore the ³⁄₈″-diameter, ½″-deep dowel holes in the bottom ends of the sides. The locations of these holes are shown in the *Side Layout*.

The face frame is also assembled with dowels. Lay out the top rail and stiles, and mark the locations of the two dowels at each joint. Using the doweling jig, drill ³⁄₈″-diameter, 1″-deep holes in the ends of the rail and edges of the stiles.

TRY THIS! If you have a plate joiner, you may also use wooden plates or "biscuits" to join the frame members.

6

Cut the shapes of the stiles and top rail. Enlarge the *Face Frame Pattern* and trace it on the stiles and top rail. Cut the shapes of the parts with a band saw or saber saw. Sand the sawed edges.

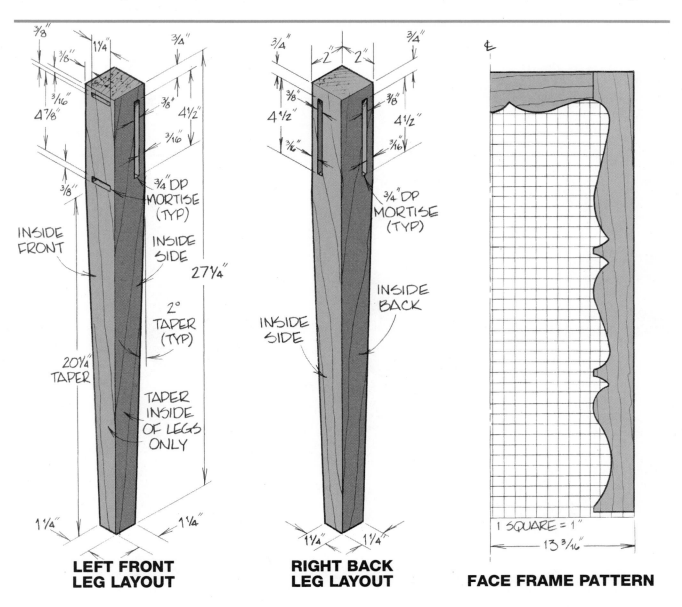

LEFT FRONT LEG LAYOUT

RIGHT BACK LEG LAYOUT

FACE FRAME PATTERN

7 Assemble the top.

Assemble the top. Finish sand the sides, shelves, stiles, and top rail. Assemble these parts in this order:

- Glue the middle and bottom shelves in the side dadoes and reinforce these joints with flathead wood screws. Drive the screws at an angle, up through each shelf and into the side, as shown in the *Shelf-to-Side Joinery Detail*.
- Glue the top shelf in the top side rabbets, and reinforce these joints with finishing nails. Drive the nails down through the shelf and into the side. Set the heads of the nails.
- Make the face frame by assembling the stiles and top rail with glue and dowels.

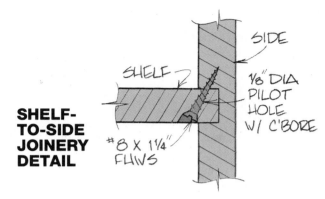

SHELF-TO-SIDE JOINERY DETAIL

- Glue the face frame assembly to the top assembly.

Let the glue dry, then sand all joints clean and flush.

8 Assemble the base.

Assemble the base. Finish sand the legs, aprons, and drawer rails. Assemble the parts in this order:

- Glue the aprons and base rails to the legs.
- Attach the spacers to the inside faces of the side aprons with glue and flathead wood screws.

- Attach the drawer guides to the inside faces of the spacers and back legs with glue and flathead wood screws.

Let the glue dry, then sand all joints clean and flush.

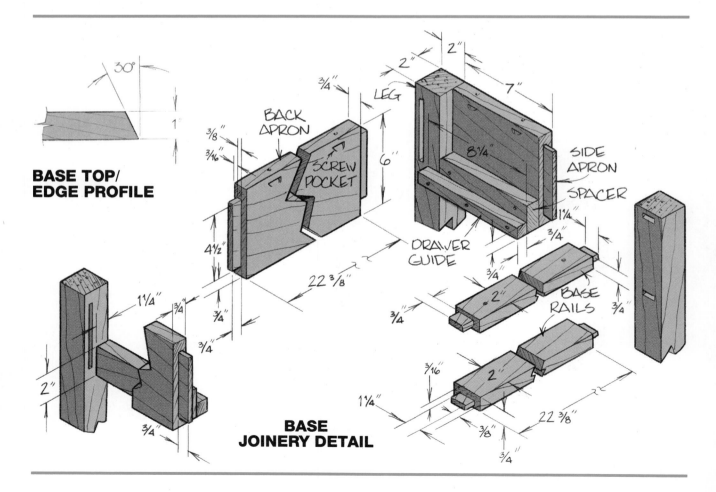

BASE TOP/ EDGE PROFILE

BASE JOINERY DETAIL

9 Join the top assembly to the base.

Finish sand the base top. Place the base top on the base, but don't screw it to the aprons or rails yet. Place dowel centers in the holes in the bottom ends of the sides. Carefully position the top assembly on the base top, and press it down firmly. The dowel centers will leave small indentations in the base top, showing you where to drill matching holes. (See Figure 2.) Remove the top assembly from the base top, then drill 3/8"-diameter, 1/2"-deep holes at each indentation.

Attach the base top to the base by driving roundhead wood screws through the screw pockets and flathead wood screws through the top base rail. Do *not* glue the base top in place.

Glue short dowels into the holes in the bottom of the top assembly, but don't glue them into the base top. Simply set the top assembly on the base top so the dowels rest in the matching holes. This will allow you to remove the top easily when you need to move the highboy.

2/Use dowel centers to lay out matching dowel holes in two wooden parts. Drill the first set of holes in one part. Place the pointed metal buttons in them. Then press the two parts together hard enough for the point of each button to leave a mark. These marks indicate the locations of holes in the other part.

10 Attach the back to the top assembly.

Cut the backboards to length, and rip each board 5–7" wide. Fit them to the back, so they rest in the rabbets. Attach them to the top shelf and sides with finishing nails. Do *not* glue them in place or attach them to the base top.

11 Attach the molding to the top assembly.

Using a table saw, bevel the edges and the back face of the molding, as shown in the *Molding Profile*. Fit the molding to the top assembly, mitering the adjoining ends at 45°. Glue the front molding to the face frame, and nail the side molding to the sides.

You can glue the mitered ends of the side molding to the front molding, but do *not* glue the side molding to the sides. The grain direction of the side molding is perpendicular to that of the sides, and if you glue the two parts together, the sides won't be able to expand and contract with changes in humidity. The sides will warp and the glue joints will eventually pop. The nails, however, bend slightly when the sides move.

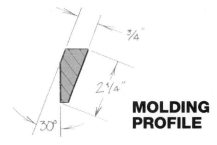

3/4"

2 1/4"

30°

MOLDING PROFILE

12 Turn the drawer pull.

Turn the wooden drawer pull to the shape shown in the *Drawer Pull Detail*. Finish sand the pull on the lathe, then drill a 1/8"-diameter, 1/2"-deep mounting hole in the back end.

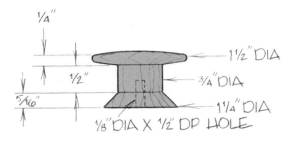

1/4"

1/2"

5/16"

1 1/2" DIA

3/4" DIA

1 1/4" DIA

1/8" DIA X 1/2" DP HOLE

DRAWER PULL DETAIL

13

Cut the drawer joinery. Measure the drawer opening to see if the dimensions have changed from what is shown in the drawings. If they have, adjust the dimensions of the drawer parts shown in the Materials List. Cut the parts — front, back, sides, and bottom. Then cut the joinery:

■ 1/2"-wide, 1/4"-deep dadoes in the drawer sides to join the back

■ 1/4"-wide, 1/4"-deep grooves in the inside faces of the front, back, and sides, as shown in the *Drawer/Side View,* to hold the bottom
■ Half-blind dovetails to join the front and sides

You can cut the dovetails by hand, or use a router and a commercial dovetail jig to make them. You may also wish to substitute simpler joinery — many country drawers just used rabbets to join the fronts and sides.

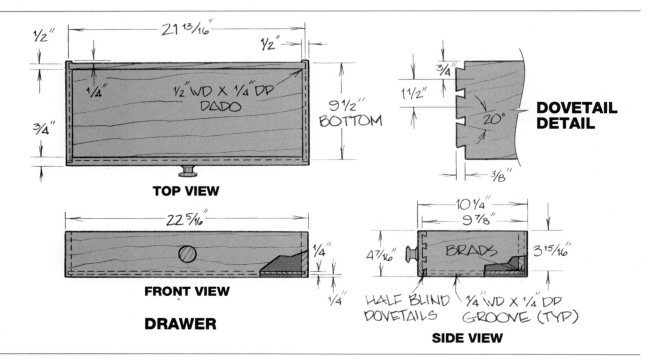

14

Assemble and fit the drawer. Dry assemble the drawer parts to test the fit of the joints. When you're satisfied that the parts fit together properly, drill a 1/8"-diameter hole for the pull through the drawer front. Then finish sand the drawer parts.

To assemble the drawer, first glue the drawer front, sides, and back together. Slide the drawer bottom into the grooves, and attach it to the drawer back with brads. *Don't* glue the bottom in place; let it float in the grooves.

Secure the drawer pull to the drawer front with a roundhead wood screw, then insert the drawer in the

base. Test the sliding action. If the drawer binds when pulled out or pushed in, remove some stock from it with a file or a plane.

TRY THIS! Some professional cabinetmakers prefer to make drawers 1/16"–1/8" oversize, then sand them down to fit precisely.

15

Apply a finish. Remove the drawer from the highboy and do any necessary touch-up sanding. Apply a finish to the completed project, coat-ing all wooden surfaces, inside and out, except the drawer sides, back, and bottom. When the finish dries, replace the drawer in the highboy.

Tilt-Back Cabinet

Country craftsmen often added their own original touches to traditional furniture forms, giving the piece a wholly new look or function. This "tilt-back" cabinet is one example.

It's a traditional cabinet — glassed-in shelves above, cupboard below, drawers in the middle. It's almost as simple and unadorned as cabinets get. Except for some molded shapes on the doors and drawers, there's little decoration. But the nineteenth-century woodworker who built it added two unusual elements: He made the back legs slightly shorter than the front, so the cabinet tilts back just 1˚; and he added extra plate grooves to the shelves, making it possible to stack the plates in front of instead of on top of each other.

This isn't an earthshaking innovation, of course. However, it neatly solves an age-old dilemma. To display the pattern on your dishes, you must display them on edge. To store a lot of the dishes in a cabinet, you have to stack them horizontally, concealing the pattern. With this tilt-back cabinet, you can store a lot of dishes *and* still see the pattern. The tilt also helps keep the door open when replacing or retrieving dinnerware.

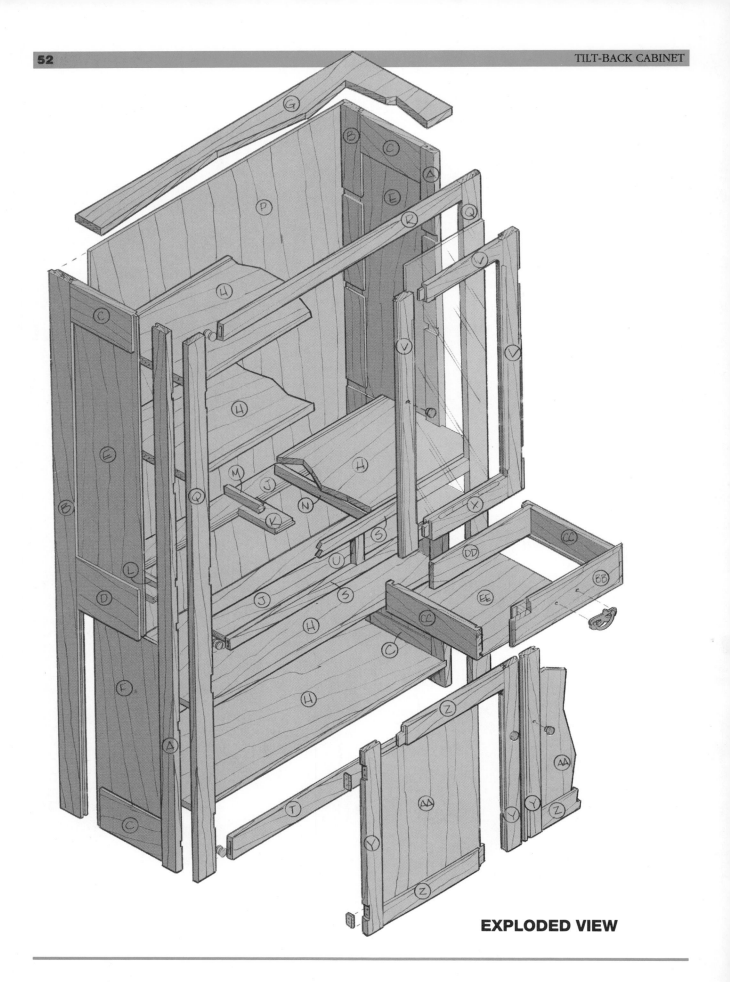

EXPLODED VIEW

Materials List

FINISHED DIMENSIONS

PARTS

A. Front side stiles (2) — 3/4" x 2" x 71 1/4"

B. Back side stiles (2) — 3/4" x 2 3/4" x 71"

C. Top/bottom side rails (4) — 3/4" x 5" x 9 3/4"

D. Middle side rails (2) — 3/4" x 7" x 9 3/4"

E. Top side panels* (2) — 1/4" x 9 5/8" x 32 1/8"

F. Bottom side panels* (2) — 1/4" x 9 5/8" x 22 5/8"

G. Top — 3/4" x 15 1/2" x 40"

H. Shelves (5) — 3/4" x 13 3/8" x 37"

J. Web frame stiles (2) — 3/4" x 3" x 37"

K. Web frame rails (3) — 3/4" x 3" x 8 1/8"

L. Left/right drawer guides (2) — 3/4" x 3/4" x 13 3/8"

M. Middle drawer guide — 3/4" x 1" x 13 3/8"

N. Kickers (4) — 3/4" x 1 1/8" x 13 3/8"

P. Back* — 3/8" x 37 1/4" x 68 1/2"

Q. Face frame stiles (2) — 3/4" x 2 3/4" x 71 1/4"

R. Top face frame rail — 3/4" x 2 1/4" x 32 1/2"

S. Middle face frame rails (2) — 3/4" x 1 1/2" x 32 1/2"

T. Bottom face frame rail — 3/4" x 2 3/4" x 32 1/2"

U. Face frame mullion — 3/4" x 1" x 4"

V. Top door stiles (4) — 3/4" x 2 1/2" x 34 1/8"

W. Top door top rails (2) — 1/2" x 2 1/2" x 13 1/2"

X. Top door bottom rails (2) — 3/4" x 2 1/2" x 13 1/2"

Y. Bottom door stiles (4) — 3/4" x 2 1/2" x 24 1/8"

Z. Bottom door rails (4) — 3/4" x 2 1/2" x 13 1/2"

AA. Bottom door panels* (2) — 1/4" x 12 1/8" x 19 3/4"

BB. Drawer fronts (2) — 3/4" x 4 11/16" x 16 7/16"

CC. Drawer sides (4) — 3/4" x 3 15/16" x 13 1/4"

DD. Drawer backs (2) — 3/4" x 3 7/16" x 14 15/16"

EE. Drawer bottoms* (2) — 1/4" x 13 1/4" x 14 15/16"

HARDWARE

#8 x 1 1/4" Flathead wood screws (21)
4d Finishing nails (1/4 lb.)
5/8" Wire brads (48–60)
#20 Wooden plates (8)
#00 Wooden plates (12)
1 1/2" x 2 1/2" Butt hinges and mounting screws (4 pairs)
Door pulls and mounting screws (4)
Door catches and mounting screws (4)
1/8" x 11 15/16" x 29 5/8" Glass panes (2)
Drawer pulls and mounting screws (2)

*These parts can be made from plywood.

1

Select the stock and cut the parts to size. To make this project, you need about 50 board feet of 4/4 (four-quarters) lumber, a 4' x 8' sheet of 3/8" cabinet-grade plywood, and one-half sheet (4' x 4') of 1/4" cabinet-grade plywood. The cabinet shown is made from oak, but you may use almost any cabinet-grade hardwood. For utilitarian projects such as these, a country cabinetmaker might have used not only oak, but also pine and poplar. If they wanted the cabinet to appear more elegant, they typically used cherry, walnut, or figured maple.

Plane about 2 board feet of the 4/4 stock to 1/2" thick, and the remainder to 3/4". Cut the case parts to size, leaving the door and drawer parts until later. These should be fitted to the assembled case. Miter the bottom ends of the side stiles and face frame stiles at 91° as shown in the *Side View*.

2

Assemble the sides and web frame. The parts of the sides and web frame are assembled with tongue-and-groove joints. Using a table-mounted router or dado cutter, make 1/4"-wide, 3/8"-deep grooves in the inside edges of the stiles, top side rails, and bottom side rails. Cut grooves in *both* edges of the middle side rails. Then cut matching tongues in the ends of all rails.

Finish sand the stiles, rails, and panels. Assemble the rails and stiles with glue. For the side assemblies, slide the panels into the grooves, but do *not* glue them in place. Let them float in the grooves. Check that the frames are square as you clamp them together.

After the glue sets up, remove the clamps and reinforce the joints with wire brads. Drive brads from the inside or underside of each frame, through each groove and into the tongue. Set the heads of the brads below the surface of the wood, but be careful the points don't protrude on the other side. Sand all the joints clean and flush.

3 Cut the joinery in the sides and top.

The case is assembled with rabbets and dadoes. Lay out the joints on the side assemblies and top, as shown in the *Front View* and *Top Layout*. Remember that the dadoes in the sides must be parallel to the *top;* the bottom is mitered at a slight angle. Cut these joints with a router or dado cutter:

- $3/8$"-wide, $3/8$"-deep rabbets in the back edges of the sides to hold the back
- $3/8$"-wide, $3/8$"-deep double-blind rabbet in the back edge of the top to hold the back. Square the blind ends with a chisel.
- $3/4$"-wide, $1/4$"-deep dadoes in the sides to hold the shelves and web frame

Note: The side dadoes should cut into the rails and stiles only; they aren't deep enough to score the panels.

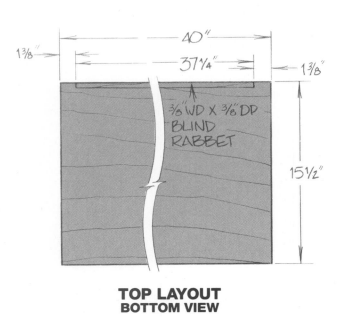

TOP LAYOUT
BOTTOM VIEW

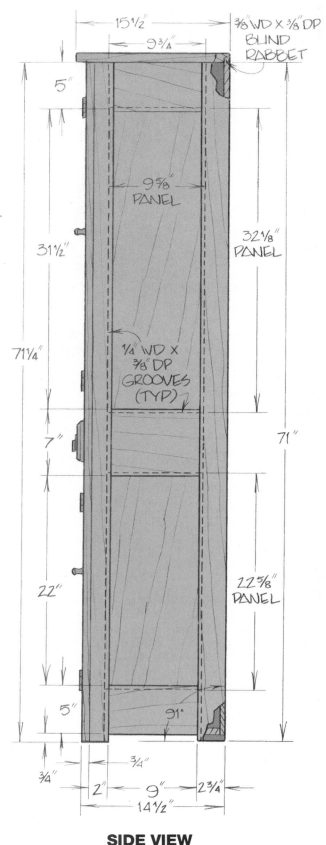

SIDE VIEW

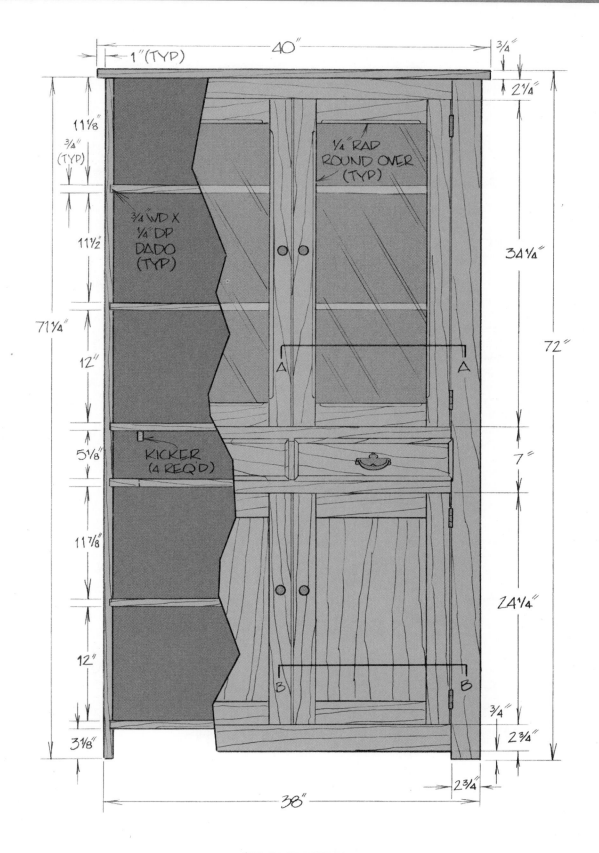

FRONT VIEW

4 ***Cut the plate grooves in the shelves.***
The ³⁄₈″-wide, ¹⁄₄″-deep grooves in the shelves hold the edges of the plates and keep them from slipping. Cut these with a router or a dado cutter. Depend-

ing on how many plates you want to store on each shelf, make a single groove, as shown in the *Shelf Section,* or several, as shown in the *Alternate Shelf Section.*

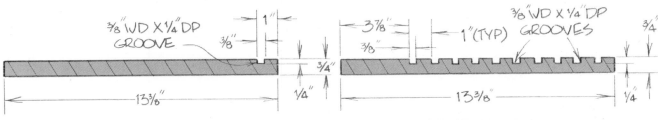

SHELF SECTION   **ALTERNATE SHELF SECTION**

5 ***Attach the kickers to the middle shelf.***
Kickers keep the drawers from tilting forward when you slide the drawers out. Counterbore and countersink three pilot holes in each kicker, as shown in the *Kicker-to-Shelf Joinery Detail.* Then screw the kickers to the underside of the middle shelf. Keep the ends of the kickers flush with the edges of the shelf. The spacing of the kickers is not critical, but there should be two kickers over each drawer in the assembled case, 12″–14″ apart.

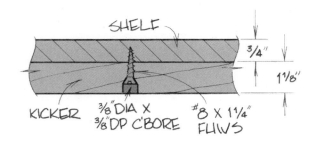

KICKER-TO-SHELF JOINERY DETAIL

6 ***Assemble the case.*** Finish sand the back, top, and shelves. Assemble the sides, shelves, and web frame with glue. (It's easier to do this with the

parts horizontal, resting on their front edges.) Make sure the assembly is square, then secure the back to it with finishing nails. Set the heads of the nails.

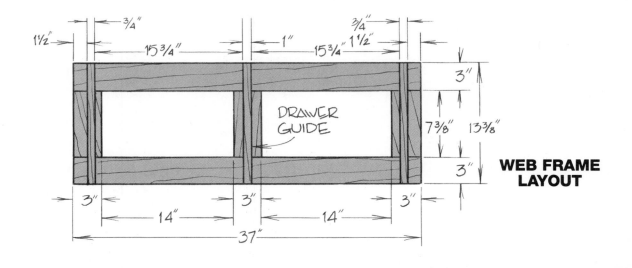

WEB FRAME LAYOUT

7 **_Attach the front frame._** With a helper, turn the case on its back. Lay out the face frame members on the front edges, and carefully mark the positions of the adjoining ends and edges on each member.

As shown in the *Face Frame Layout,* the members are joined with wooden plates or "biscuits." However, you can also use dowels. If you wish to use biscuits, cut slots in the adjoining ends and edges with a plate joiner. If you prefer dowels, drill dowel holes, using a doweling jig to guide the bit.

Finish sand the face frame members. Assemble the members with glue and biscuits (or dowels). Before the glue sets up, glue the face frame to the front edges of the case and clamp it in place. After the glue dries, sand all joints clean and flush.

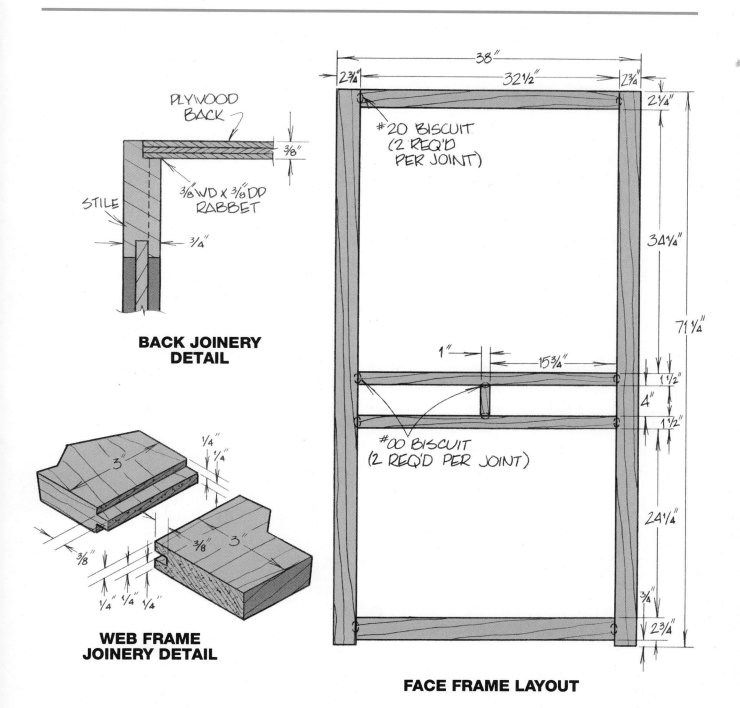

BACK JOINERY DETAIL

WEB FRAME JOINERY DETAIL

FACE FRAME LAYOUT

8 **Attach the drawer guides to the web frame.** Glue the drawer guides to the web frame. The edges of the guides must be perpendicular to the front edge of the web frame, and flush with the inside edges of the face frame members. Reinforce the glue joints by driving flathead wood screws up through the web frame and into the guides.

9 **Cut the door and drawer parts.** Carefully measure the opening in the case for the doors and drawers. These may have changed slightly from what is shown in the drawings — this is common with large projects. If necessary, adjust the dimensions shown in the Materials List, then cut the parts to size.

10 **Cut the lips on the drawer fronts.** The drawer fronts have lips that overlap the face frame members. To make the lips, cut ³⁄₈″-wide, ³⁄₈″- deep rabbets in the edges and ends of the stock, as shown in the *Drawer Lip Profile*.

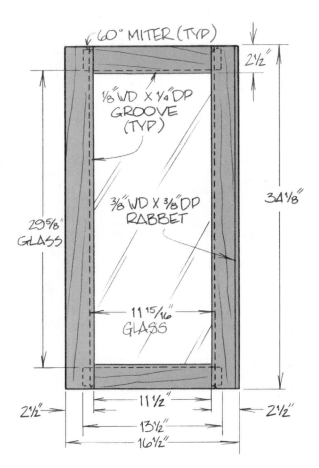

TOP DOOR LAYOUT
BACK VIEW

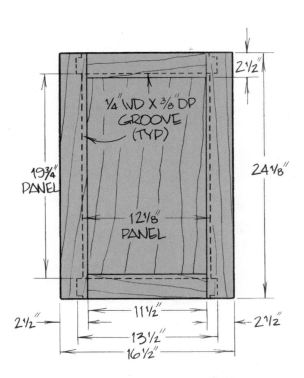

BOTTOM DOOR LAYOUT

11

Cut the drawer joinery. Like the case, the parts of the drawers are assembled with simple joinery. Using a router or a dado cutter, make these dadoes and grooves:

- ³/₄"-wide, ³/₈"-deep dadoes in the sides to hold the drawer backs
- ¹/₄"-wide, ³/₈"-deep grooves in the drawer fronts and sides to hold the bottoms

- ³/₁₆"-wide, ³/₈"-deep dadoes, ³/₁₆" from the front ends of the drawer sides
- ³/₁₆"-wide, ³/₄"-deep grooves in the ends of the drawer fronts (as measured from the cheek of the rabbet). These will create ³/₁₆"-wide tongues. Trim these tongues to ³/₈" long, so they will interlock with the dadoes in the sides.

12

Cut coves in the drawer lips. With a router and a ³/₈" cove bit, cut coves in the lips on the drawer fronts. This is shown in the *Drawer Lip Profile*. Sand the lips to remove mill marks.

Note: You may rout other shapes instead of coves, if you wish. Traditionally, drawer lips are rounded over with a quarter-round bit.

13

Assemble and fit the drawers. Finish sand the drawer parts, then assemble the fronts, sides, and backs with glue. Slide the bottoms into the grooves, but do *not* glue them to the other drawer parts. Let them float in the grooves. Secure them to the backs with brads.

Let the glue dry, then sand the drawer joints clean. Attach drawer pulls to the fronts. Insert the drawers in the case, then slide them in and out several times. If they bind or seem tight, sand or plane a little stock from the sides and back until they slide smoothly.

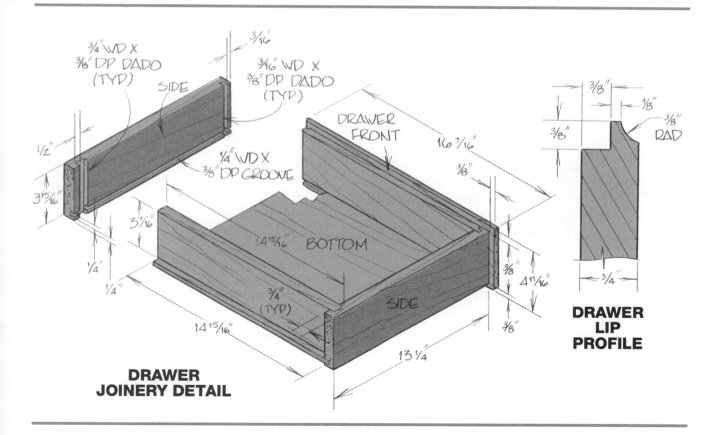

DRAWER JOINERY DETAIL

DRAWER LIP PROFILE

14 Cut the door joinery.

Both the top and the bottom door frames are joined with mortises and tenons. However, the bottom frame members are grooved to hold wooden panels, and the top frame members are grooved to hold glass panels. Make the joints in this order:

- Using a table saw and an ordinary saw blade, cut ⅛″-wide, ¼″-deep grooves in the inside edges of the top door stiles and top door bottom rails. This is shown in the *Top Door Joinery Detail*.
- Switching to a table-mounted router or dado cutter, cut ⅜″-wide, ⅜″-deep rabbets on the outside edges of the middle stiles, as shown in *Section A* and *Section B*.
- Cut ¼″-wide, ⅜″-deep grooves in the inside edges of the bottom door rails and stiles, as shown in the *Bottom Door Joinery Detail*. (See Figure 1.)

- Cut ¼″-thick, 1″-long tenons on the ends of all the rails. (See Figure 2.)
- Using a drill and a mortising chisel, make ¼″-wide, 1½″-long, 1″-deep mortises in the inside edges of the top door stiles, ½″ from each end.
- Cut ¼″-wide, 1¾″-long, 1″-deep mortises in the inside edges of the bottom door stiles, ⅜″ from each end. (See Figure 3.)
- With a band saw or dovetail saw, notch the shoulders of the tenons to fit the mortises. (See Figure 4.)
- Using a back saw or dovetail saw, cut 60° miters in the inside face of the top door stiles, near the top and bottom ends, as shown in the *Top Door Joinery Detail*. These miters prevent the thin tongues (created when you cut the glass grooves) from catching and splitting as you open and close the doors.

1/To join the door parts, first cut the grooves in the inside edges of the frame members. The grooves in the top door are just ⅛″ wide, while those in the bottom door (shown) are ¼″ wide.

2/Cut ¼″-thick tenons on the ends of the door rails. Use a tenoning jig to hold the wood as you cut.

3/Make the mortises in the stiles by drilling a series of overlapping holes. Each mortise should be as wide as the adjoining tenon is thick. Clean up the edges and square the ends of the mortises with a chisel.

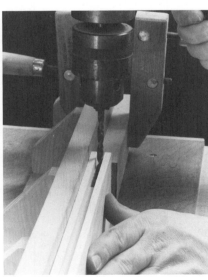

*4/Using a band saw or dovetail saw, cut notches or **haunches** in the shoulders of the tenons, fitting them to the mortises. The fit should be snug, but not too tight.*

15 Cut beads in the edges of the door stiles.

Using a molder and a beading knife, or a router and a point-cut quarter-round bit, cut $3/16''$ beads in the door stiles, as shown in *Section A* and *Section B*. Make a single, long bead in the outside edge of each right outside door stile, left outside door stile, and right middle door stile.

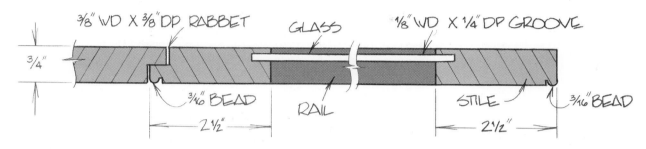

SECTION A

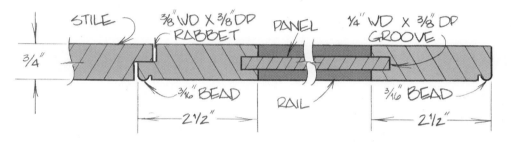

SECTION B

16 Assemble the doors.

Finish sand all the door parts. Glue the rails and stiles together, inserting the tenons in the mortises. Slide the bottom door panels into the grooves, but do *not* glue them in place. Let them float in the grooves.

17 Round over the inside edges of the door frames.

As shown in the *Front View,* the edges of the front stiles are rounded over. Cut these shapes with a router and a piloted $3/8''$ quarter-round bit. Don't try to rout into the corners.

18 Mount the doors.

Mortise the face frame stiles and outside door stiles for hinges, then mount the doors in the case. Install door pulls on the doors and catches inside the case.

19

Apply a finish to the cabinet and install the glass. Remove the doors, drawers, and hardware from the case. Do any necessary touch-up sanding, then apply a finish to all wooden surfaces, inside and out, except the drawer sides, backs, and bottoms.

When the finish dries, replace the doors, drawers, and hardware. Slide the panes of glass into the grooves in the top doors. There's no need for glazing strips or glazing compound — gravity will prevent the glass from falling out of the frame.

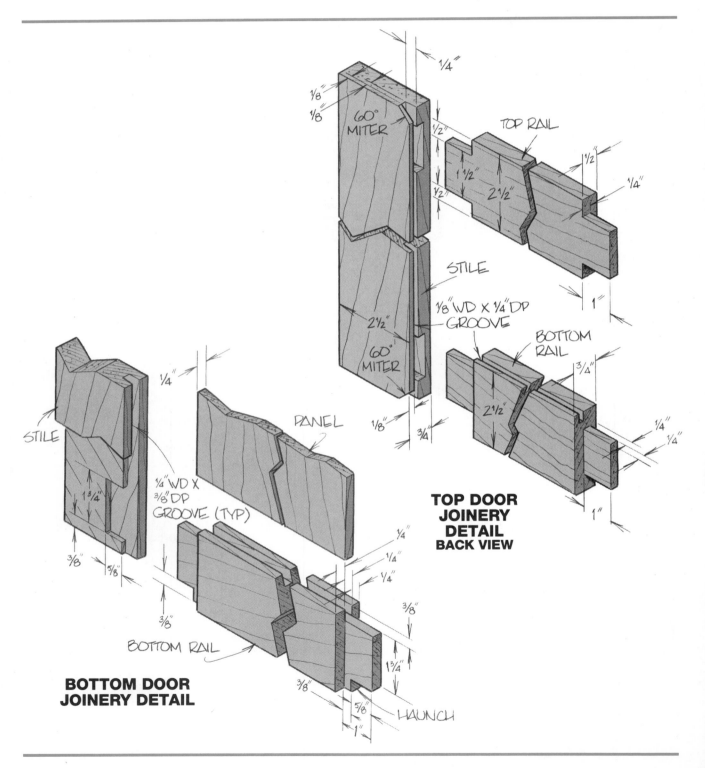

TOP DOOR JOINERY DETAIL
BACK VIEW

BOTTOM DOOR JOINERY DETAIL

Dish Dresser

The word "dresser" evolved from the old French word *dressoir,* meaning to set or arrange. The country dish dresser evolved from a simple medieval side table on which a cook "dressed" (set or arranged) food before serving it. In the early seventeenth century, country craftsmen began to build sets of shelves (or cup-boards) above their dressers to hold dishes between meals. During the next century they enclosed the bottom, creating a storage cabinet for table linens. By the late 1700s, the dish dresser had acquired the traditional form shown here.

This dresser is typical of *primitive* American furniture — pieces built by rural craftsmen with limited woodworking tools and experience. There is no fancy joinery; all the parts are assembled with butt joints and nailed together. However, this simplicity doesn't detract from the dresser's strength or appearance. It still exudes country charm, and it will for centuries, like many of its primitive ancestors.

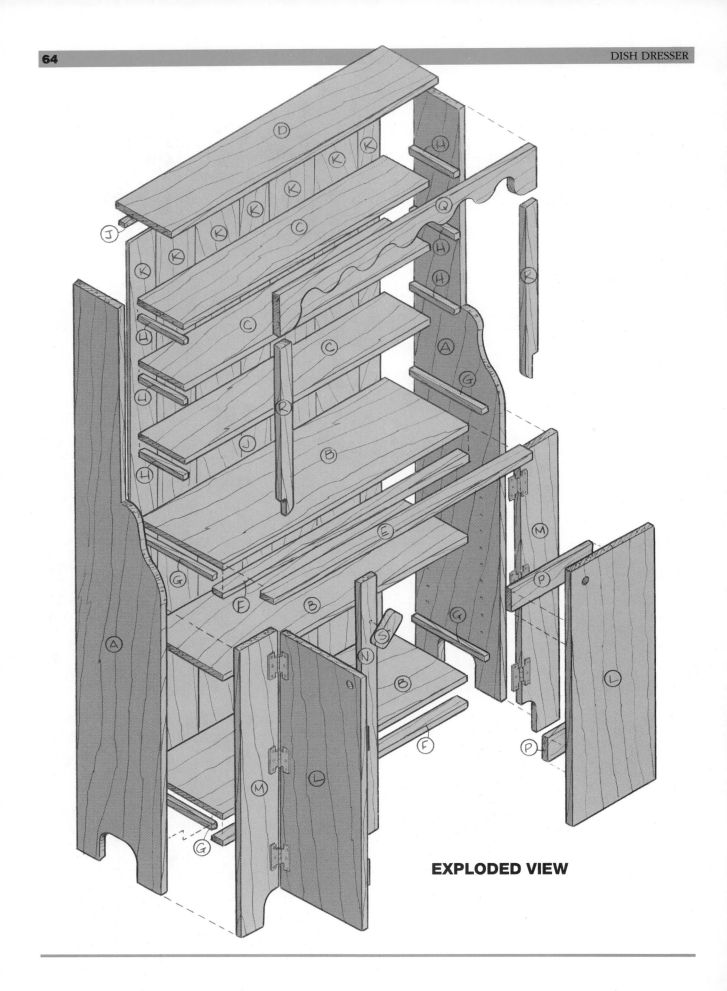

EXPLODED VIEW

Materials List

FINISHED DIMENSIONS

PARTS

A. Sides (2) ³/₄″ x 11¹/₄″ x 67¹/₄″
B. Bottom shelves/
counter (3) ³/₄″ x 10⁷/₈″ x 33″
C. Top shelves (3) ³/₄″ x 5⁵/₈″ x 33″
D. Top ³/₄″ x 7¹/₂″ x 36″
E. Counter front ³/₄″ x 1¹/₂″ x 34¹/₂″
F. Shelf braces (2) ³/₄″ x 1¹/₂″ x 31¹/₂″
G. Bottom shelf
cleats (4) ³/₄″ x ³/₄″ x 10⁷/₈″
H. Top shelf
cleats (6) ³/₄″ x ³/₄″ x 5⁵/₈″

J. Back cleat ³/₄″ x ³/₄″ x 33″
K. Backboards
(5–7) ³/₈″ x (variable) x 63¹/₄″
L. Doors (2) ³/₄″ x 11³/₈″ x 30³/₁₆″
M. Bottom stiles (2) ³/₄″ x 4³/₄″ x 34¹/₄″
N. Door stile ³/₄″ x 2″ x 30¹/₄″
P. Door braces (4) ³/₄″ x 3″ x 10³/₄″
Q. Valance ³/₄″ x 5″ x 34¹/₂″
R. Top stiles (2) ³/₄″ x 1¹/₂″ x 20¹/₄″
S. Turnbutton ³/₄″ x 1¹/₂″ x 4″

HARDWARE

⁷/₈″ Wire or headless brads (40–50)
4d Finishing or headless square-cut
nails (¹/₂ lb.)
6d Square-cut nails (¹/₂ lb.)
#10 x 1¹/₄″ Roundhead wood screws
(13)
#10 Flat washers (13)
3″ Black H-hinges and mounting
screws (3 pair)
¹/₄″ Pin-style shelving supports (4)

1 **Choose the materials, and cut the parts to size.** Country craftsmen made dressers from white pine or poplar, if they were meant to be painted or stained, and woods like cherry or walnut if they were left natural. This particular dresser is designed to be made from ordinary pine stock, which you can buy at any lumberyard. Make sure you select premium or #1 *kiln-dried* wood. Lesser grades are not well dried,

and they may shrink, warp, or split after you build the dresser.

You'll need approximately 45 board feet of stock. If you can, purchase enough 12″-wide stock to make the sides and bottom shelves. If you can't, glue up the widths needed. Then cut all the parts to size, except one backboard. Cut this to the proper thickness and length, but wait to rip it to width.

2 **Shape the parts.** Most of the pieces in the dish dresser are simple rectangles, as you can see from the *Exploded View*. However, you must cut several shapes — the sides, bottom stiles, top stiles, and valance.

Enlarge the *Valance Pattern* and the *Side, Top Stile, and Bottom Stile Patterns*. Trace the shapes on the stock, then cut them out, using a band saw, saber saw, or a coping saw. Sand the sawed edges smooth.

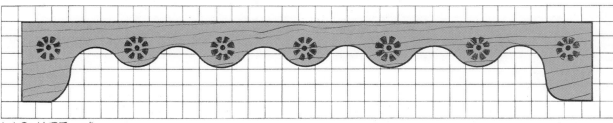

1 SQUARE = 1″

VALANCE PATTERN

3 **Drill the finger holes in the doors.**
There are no door pulls on this dresser. The pioneers and settlers who made primitive furniture rarely had extra money to spend on hardware. So most drawers and doors had simple wooden knobs or finger holes, as shown. Mark the position of the finger hole on each door, then drill a 1″-diameter hole through the board. Round over the edges and smooth the inside of the hole with a half-round rasp and file.

TRY THIS! If you have one, use a Forstner or multispur bit to drill the finger holes. Both of these cut holes with exceptionally smooth sides.

4 **Drill the shelf-support holes in the sides.**   The middle bottom shelf is adjustable, and rests on movable pegs. These pegs fit in ¼″-diameter holes in the sides. Mark the positions of the holes on the *inside* face of each side, as shown in the *Side, Top Stile, and Bottom Stile Patterns,* then drill each hole ½″ deep.

5 **Assemble the dish dresser.**   Finish sand the parts, then assemble them in the following order, using glue and nails:

■ First, attach the bottom and top shelf cleats to the sides with 4d nails. Make sure the ends of the cleats are flush with the *front* edges of the sides. (They should be ³⁄₈″ from the *back* edges.)

■ Using glue and 4d nails, attach one shelf brace to the bottom surface of the counter, and the other to the bottom shelf. The front edges of the braces must be flush with these parts. Also, the braces should be centered side-to-side under the shelf or counter.

■ Glue the counter front to the counter, edge to edge. Center the counter front side-to-side on the counter.

■ Using glue and 4d nails, attach the back cleat to the bottom surface of the top. The cleat should be centered side-to-side, and its back edge should be ³⁄₈″ from the back edge of the top.

■ Attach the top, counter, top shelves, and bottom shelf to the cleats with 4d nails.

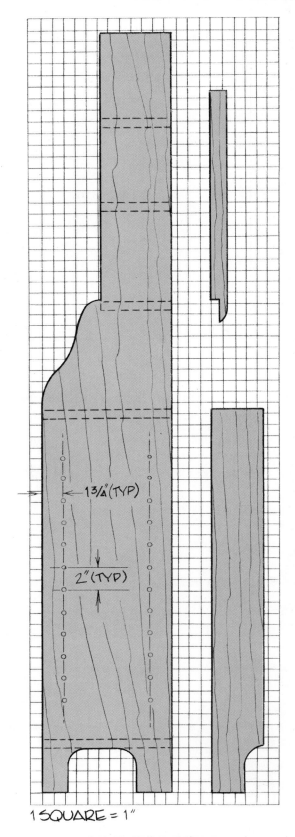

1 SQUARE = 1″

**SIDE, TOP STILE,
AND BOTTOM STILE PATTERNS**

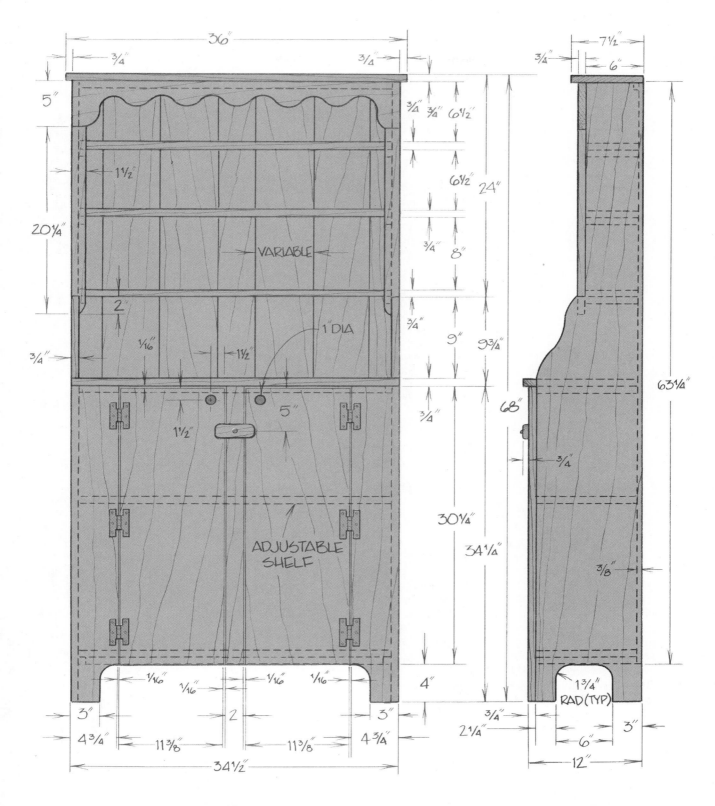

FRONT VIEW

SIDE VIEW

■ Lay the dresser assembly on its front edges. Using a try-square or carpenter's square, make certain that the shelves and counter are square to the sides. (The assembly won't be rigid until you add the backboards — the joints between the sides and shelves should flex easily.) When the dresser is square, attach the backboards with ⅞″ brads. Do *not* glue these boards in place, just nail them to the top cleat, shelves, and counter. Leave a ¹⁄₁₆″–⅛″ gap between each board to allow for expansion and contraction. Carefully measure the space left for the last backboard, rip it to the width needed, and tack it in place.

■ Turn the assembly over on its back and attach the valance, top stiles, door stile, and bottom stiles with glue and 6d nails.

As you work, be careful that the nails don't go completely through the wood. The 4d nails are 1½″ long — long enough that the points may protrude when you drive them through two ¾″-thick boards. To prevent this, drive them at steep angles. (See Figure 1.)

Use a wet rag to wipe away any glue that squeezes out of the joints. When the glue dries, set the heads of the nails slightly below the surface of the wood with a nail punch. Sand all the joints clean and the surfaces flush.

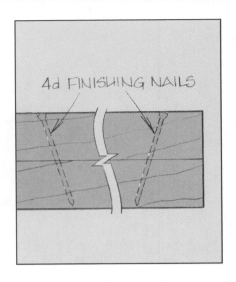

1/When you join two pieces of ¾″-thick stock, the 4d nails are long enough to go completely through the wood. To prevent this, drive the nails at angles. Vary the angles back and forth — this helps "hook" the parts together.

TRY THIS! If you wish, use *cut nails* or *hand-wrought nails* instead of regular store-bought nails. These have square shanks and imitate the look of hand-forged nails — the only nails available to most early nineteenth-century country craftsmen. This, in turn, helps to make the project more authentic.

6 Hang the doors. Before you can mount the doors on the dresser, you must brace the doors so they don't cup or warp. However, you must also allow them to expand and contract with changes in temperature and humidity. If you simply nail or glue braces to the back side of the doors, the results will be worse than if you had used no braces at all. The doors may begin to warp or split almost immediately.

To brace the doors *and* allow for the natural movement of the wood, attach the braces by driving screws through oversize holes. Drill ⁵⁄₁₆″-diameter pilot holes through the braces, and ⅛″-diameter pilot holes in the doors. Place flat washers on #10 x 1¼″ roundhead wood screws, then drive them through the braces and into the doors. Tighten the screws so they're snug, but not so tight that the washers bite into the wood.

Position each door in its opening. (The dresser should still be laying down.) Arrange the door so there is a ¹⁄₁₆″ gap at the top and on each side, between the door and the dresser assembly. Place the hinges on the door, and mark the positions of the mounting screws. Drill pilot holes for the screws, and attach the hinges. Open and close the door several times to make sure it doesn't bind or rub.

TRY THIS! Just as square-shanked nails add authenticity to this project, so will hand-forged *rat-tail hinges*. These primitive hinges were much easier for a country blacksmith to make than butt hinges, consequently they were much less expensive. You can still purchase these hinges from:

Ball and Ball
463 W. Lincoln Highway
Exton, PA 19341

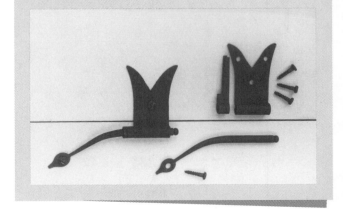

7 Attach the turnbutton.

Attach the turnbutton. Drill a ¼″-diameter hole through the center of the turnbutton, as shown in the *Turnbutton Layout*. Put a flat washer on the #10 x 1¼″ roundhead screw, and insert the screw through the hole in the turnbutton. Fasten the turn-button to the middle stile, about 5″ below the counter, in the same manner that you fastened the braces to the doors. When the turnbutton is horizontal, it holds the doors closed. To open the doors, turn it so it's vertical.

8 Paint or finish the dish dresser.

Paint or finish the dish dresser. Remove the doors and turnbutton from the completed dresser. Also remove the hinges from the doors. Set the hardware aside and lightly sand the wooden surfaces clean.

Stain and finish, or paint the dresser. If you paint, you may also wish to add a stenciled ornament to the valance, as shown. Enlarge the *Stencil Pattern* and make a stencil template. Using this template, apply the stencil in a color that contrasts with — yet compliments — the color of the dresser. When the paint or finish dries, replace the doors and hardware. Also install the shelving supports and adjustable shelf.

Note: Apply as many coats of paint or finish to the inside surface of the dresser as you do to the outside. This will help keep the finished piece from splitting or distorting over time.

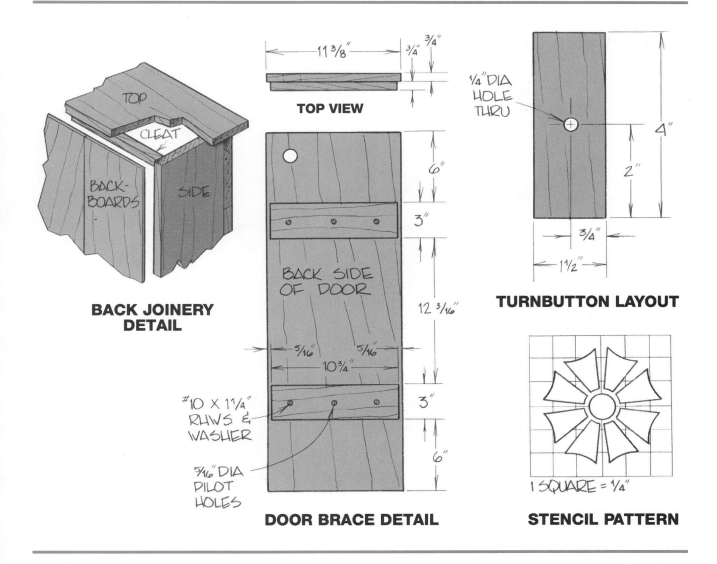

BACK JOINERY DETAIL

TOP VIEW

DOOR BRACE DETAIL

TURNBUTTON LAYOUT

STENCIL PATTERN

Shaker Candle Ledge

Not all country shelves were mounted to the wall or set on the floor. Craftsmen designed some small pieces, like this candle ledge, to be moved from place to place. This particular ledge, patterned after a Shaker design from Hancock, Massachusetts, could be easily hung on (or removed from) a peg. Since the Shakers typically lined the rooms of their community buildings with peg rails, they could use the ledge in any room. They carried the candle and ledge from room to room, hanging it on the wall wherever they wished.

More often, they moved the candle ledge around within a single room. Since they could place it anywhere there was a peg, and hang it at several different heights, a Shaker brother or sister could set the candle where its light was most needed. They might also use the ledge to hold other small items — kitchen utensils, sewing notions, tools, a water glass, or the personal effects that folks collect in their pockets.

Today, you might use this ledge to hold plants, spice jars, or collectibles. If you wish, build several ledges, varying the length, width, or depth. Hang these on a peg rail to create a movable shelving system.

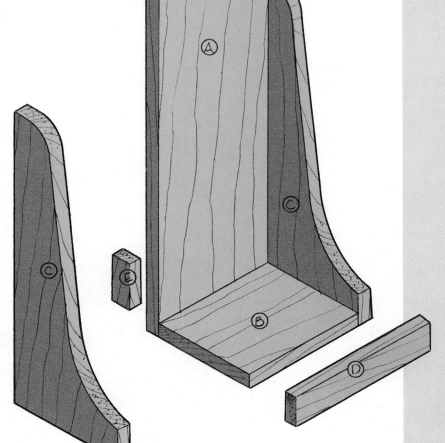

EXPLODED VIEW

Materials List
FINISHED DIMENSIONS

PARTS

A. Back $1/2'' \times 5^{1/4}'' \times 22^{3/4}''$
B. Bottom $1/2'' \times 4^{1/2}'' \times 6''$
C. Sides (2) $1/2'' \times 5'' \times 12^{1/2}''$
D. Front $1/2'' \times 1^{1/4}'' \times 7^{1/16}''$
E. Spacers (2) $1/2'' \times 3/4'' \times 2''$

HARDWARE

1″ Wire or headless brads (16–24)

1 Select the materials and cut the parts to size.

Craftsmen made small pieces like these out of many different types of wood, but they preferred white pine. The reason was pine's workability — in an age before power planers, it was much easier to work a soft, close-grained wood like pine down to ½″ thick than it was harder woods. Pine is also surprisingly durable for a softwood. The ledge shown is made from this wood.

To make this project, you'll need approximately 3 board feet of 4/4 (four-quarters) wood planed to ½″ thick. Cut the parts to the sizes given in the Materials List. Bevel the ends of the front and the edges of the back and sides, as shown in the *Top View*.

2 Drill the mounting holes in the back.

Lay out the locations of the three mounting holes — the holes used to hang the ledge from a peg — on the back. Drill the 1¼″-diameter holes through the stock. Sand the inside edges of the holes smooth.

TRY THIS! If you have Forstner or multi-spur bits, use them to make the holes. Both of these drilling tools make exceptionally smooth cuts.

3 Cut the shapes of the back and sides.

Lay out the shapes of the back and sides, as shown on the *Front View* and *Side View*. Cut the parts with a band saw or scroll saw, then sand the sawed edges.

4 Assemble the ledge.

Finish sand all the parts, then assemble them with glue and brads. When the glue dries, sand all the joints clean and flush. Round the edges and corners with a rasp or file, and set the heads of the brads.

TRY THIS! You can hide the heads of the brads with a *blind nail plane*. Using the plane, lift a small curl of wood wherever you need to drive a brad. Drive the brad through the groove left by the plane, set the head, then glue the curl back in the groove. Let the glue dry, and sand the surface smooth. You won't be able to tell there's a brad just under the surface of the wood.

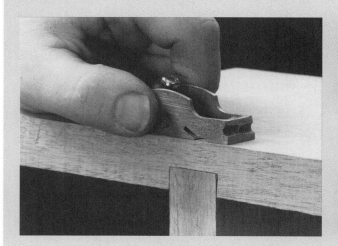

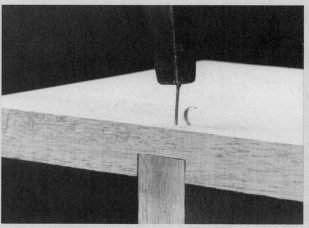

5 **Finish the project.** Do any necessary touch-up sanding on the completed ledge, then apply a finish. To make the ledge appear worn, sand away some of the finish at the front corners and around the mounting holes.

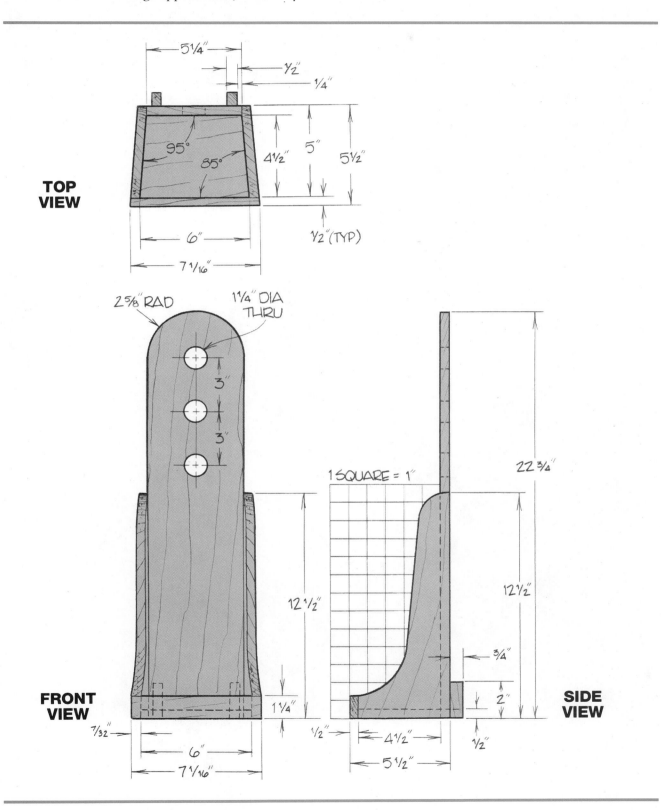

Child's Hutch

C ountry folks occasionally made miniature furniture. Itinerant craftsmen or salesmen used these miniatures to show off their wares. Cabinetmakers made miniature prototypes to get the clients' approval before building full-size pieces. But most miniatures were made for children to play with.

This miniature hutch probably had an important place in the make-believe kitchen of a young girl in the early nineteenth century. It's made simply, but surprisingly well for toy furniture. Considering the caliber of the craftsmanship, it could have been built by a doting father or grandfather who ran a cabinetmaking shop.

Today, these miniatures are attracting adults as well as children. Young people continue to use them for what they've always been used for — "just pretend." However, collectors and other adults who appreciate country furniture have begun to use them to store jewelry, or to display small items.

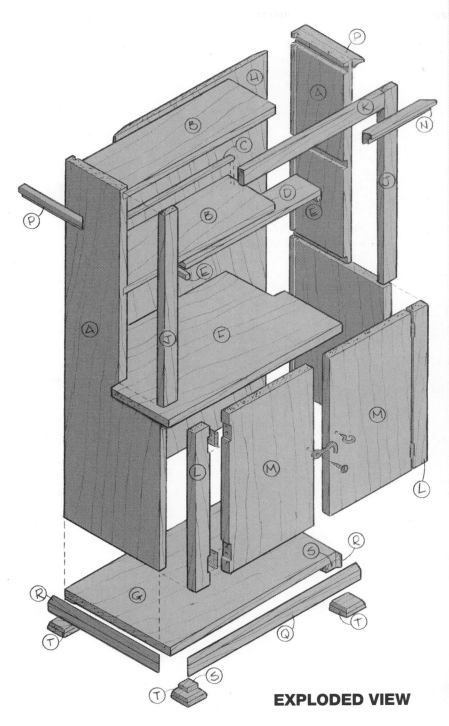

EXPLODED VIEW

Materials List
FINISHED DIMENSIONS

PARTS

A.	Sides	1/2" x 7" x 23 1/2"
B.	Top shelves (2)	1/2" x 3 3/4" x 12 1/8"
C.	Plate holder	1/4" x 1/2" x 11 5/8"
D.	Half shelf	1/2" x 2 1/2" x 11 5/8"
E.	Cleats (2)	1/2" x 1/2" x 2 1/2"
F.	Counter	1/2" x 7 1/2" x 13 5/8"
G.	Bottom	1/2" x 7 1/2" x 12 5/8"
H.	Back	1/4" x 12" x 23 1/2"
J.	Top stiles (2)	1/2" x 1" x 12 1/2"
K.	Top rail	1/2" x 1" x 10 5/8"
L.	Bottom stiles (2)	1/2" x 1" x 10 1/2"
M.	Doors (2)	1/2" x 5 7/32" x 10 3/8"
N.	Front top molding	1/2" x 3/4" x 13 5/8"
P.	Side top moldings (2)	1/2" x 3/4" x 5"
Q.	Front bottom molding	3/16" x 3/4" x 13"
R.	Side bottom molding	3/16" x 3/4" x 7 11/16"
S.	Spacers (4)	1/4" x 1" x 1 3/8"
T.	Feet (4)	1/2" x 1 1/4" x 1 5/8"

HARDWARE

1" x 1 1/2" Butt hinges and mounting
  screws (2 pairs)
Small hook and eye
2d Square-cut nails (42–48)
5/8" Wire brads (10–12)

1

Select the stock and cut the parts to size. To build this project, you'll need approximately 8 board feet of 4/4 (four-quarters) lumber. The hutch shown is made of poplar, but country craftsmen also used white pine for painted pieces. If they planned to finish a piece with a clear varnish or shellac, they might have also used cherry, walnut, or figured maple.

After you've chosen the stock, plane most of it to ½″ thick. You'll also need a scrap (less than ¼ board foot) of ¾″-thick stock to make the bottom moldings, and an even smaller scrap of ¼″-thick stock for the spacers. Cut all the parts to the sizes specified in the Materials List, except the top and bottom moldings. Wait to fit these to the assembled hutch.

2

Cut the joinery in the sides. The case is assembled with simple dadoes and grooves. Using a router or a dado cutter, cut ½″-wide, ¼″-deep dadoes in the sides. Then, with a table saw and an

ordinary combination blade, cut a ⅛″-wide, ¼″-deep groove near the back edge. All these joints are shown in the *Side Layout*.

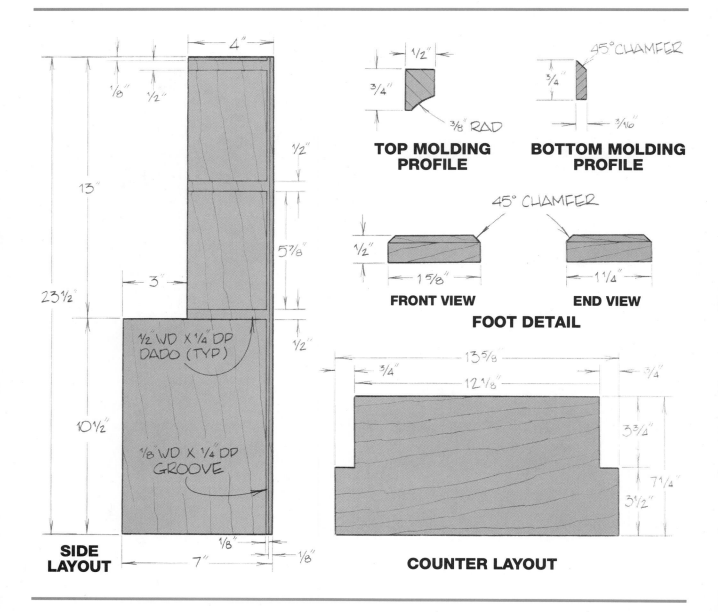

SIDE LAYOUT

TOP MOLDING PROFILE

BOTTOM MOLDING PROFILE

FOOT DETAIL

FRONT VIEW   END VIEW

COUNTER LAYOUT

3 **Cut the shapes of the sides and counter.** Lay out the shapes of the sides and counter, as shown in the *Side Layout* and *Counter Layout*. Cut them with a band saw or saber saw.

4 **Fit the back to the grooves in the sides.** To make the ¼″-thick back fit in the ⅛″-wide grooves in the sides, chamfer its edges with a small hand plane, as shown in the *Top View*. Cut these chamfers on the back surface.

5 **Assemble the case.** Finish sand the sides, shelves, half shelf, counter, bottom, back, stiles, and rail. Assemble the parts in the following order:

- Glue the cleats to the sides, as shown in the *Side View*.
- Glue the shelves and counter in the side dadoes. Reinforce the joints with square-cut nails, driving the nails through the sides and into the ends of the shelves and counter.

- Glue the bottom to the sides, and reinforce the joints with nails.
- Slide the back into the side grooves. Nail (but do *not* glue) it to the shelves and counter.
- Glue the top rail to the top shelf, and the top stiles and bottom stiles to the sides.

After the glue dries, sand all joints clean and flush. Set the heads of the nails. If you wish, cover the heads with putty.

6 **Attach the moldings.** Select a board ½″ thick and at least 3″ wide for the molding stock. With a router or shaper, cut a ⅜″-radius cove in the edge of the top molding stock, as shown in the *Top Molding Profile*. Rip the molding from the wide board. Follow the same procedure to make the bottom molding: Cut a 45° chamfer in the top corner of a wide board, as shown in the *Bottom Molding Profile,* then rip the molding from the board. (See Figure 1.)

Fit the moldings to the case, mitering the adjoining ends at 45°. Finish sand the molding parts after you cut them. Glue the front moldings to the case, and attach the side moldings with small brads. You can glue the front ends of the side moldings to the case, but the remainder should be secured with nails *only*. This will allow the sides to expand and contract with changes

*1/When making narrow moldings, always shape the edge of a wide board, **then** rip the molding from the stock. Never try to shape slender stock. It may kick back or come apart as you feed it into the router or shaper.*

in humidity. As the wood moves, the nails will bend slightly. If you glue the moldings to the sides, this movement will be restricted. Eventually, the sides will warp or cup, and the glue joints will pop.

7 **Attach the feet to the case.** Using a hand plane or a small chisel, cut chamfers in the tops of the feet, as shown in the *Foot Detail*. Glue spacers to the bottom, one at each corner. (The bottom surface of the spacers must be flush with the bottom edge of the bottom molding.) Then glue the feet to the spacers.

8 **Mount the doors.** Mortise the doors and bottom stiles for hinges. Finish sand the doors, then mount them in the case. Attach a hook and eye to keep them closed, as shown in the *Front View*.

9 **Finish the hutch.** Remove the doors from the hutch, and the hardware from the doors. Apply paint or a finish to all wooden surfaces — inside and out, top and bottom. After the finish dries, replace the doors and hardware.

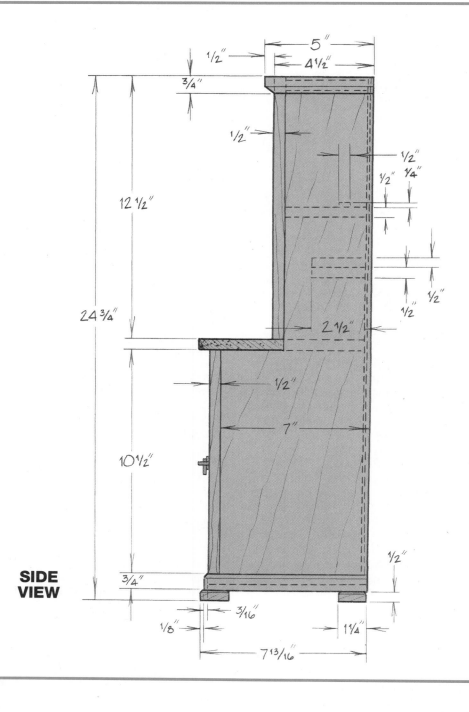

SIDE
VIEW

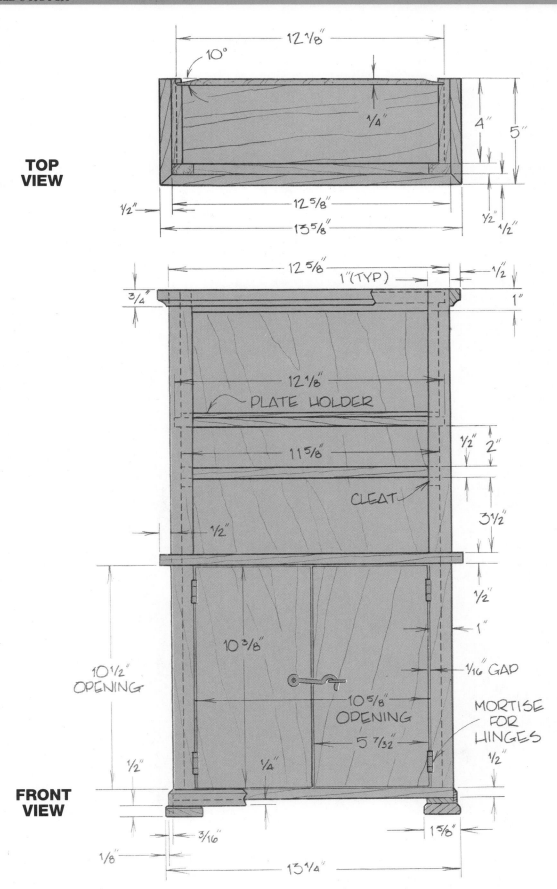

TOP VIEW

12⅛"

10°

¼"

4"

5"

½"

12⅝"

15⅝"

½"

½"

FRONT VIEW

12⅝"

1"(TYP)

½"

¾"

1"

12⅛"

PLATE HOLDER

½" 2"

11⅝"

CLEAT

3½"

½"

½"

1"

10⅜"

1/16" GAP

10½" OPENING

MORTISE FOR HINGES

10⅝" OPENING

5 7/32"

½"

½"

¼"

3/16"

1⅝"

⅛"

13¼"

Hanging Corner Cupboard

Corner furniture — triangular shelves, cupboards, tables, and chairs designed to fit in a corner — was popular in country homes. Eighteenth- and nineteenth-century rural homes were usually small, while families were large. Consequently, folks couldn't afford to waste an inch of space. So when the walls and floors were full of furniture, they began to use the corners.

The cupboard shown was made to hang in a corner, possibly filling the space above a table or chair. Folks might use it in any room to store all sorts of small and medium-size items — kitchen utensils, spices, liquor, linens, clothes, tools, and so on. Now and then, craftsmen built these hanging corner pieces with glass doors to display china or keepsakes. The small "scroll shelf" below the cupboard was an aesthetic touch. If the piece was used as a spice cupboard, the cook might set a salt box on this shelf. Otherwise, the scroll shelf was more decorative than practical.

This particular cupboard was built without a solid back — there are no panels between the stiles that support the shelves. This reduces the materials needed, making the cupboard less expensive and easier to build. It also reduces the weight, making the cupboard easier to hang.

EXPLODED VIEW

Materials List

FINISHED DIMENSIONS

PARTS

A. Top/
bottom (2) $\frac{3}{4}$" x 17$\frac{11}{16}$" x 30$\frac{3}{4}$"

B. Adjustable
shelves (1–2) $\frac{3}{4}$" x 16$\frac{3}{16}$" x 28$\frac{5}{8}$"

C. Scroll shelf $\frac{3}{4}$" x 6" x 8$\frac{1}{2}$"

D. Right back stile $\frac{3}{4}$" x 11$\frac{1}{4}$" x 47$\frac{1}{4}$"

E. Left back stile $\frac{3}{4}$" x 12" x 47$\frac{1}{4}$"

F. Corner stiles (2) $\frac{3}{4}$" x 2$\frac{1}{4}$" x 34$\frac{1}{2}$"

G. Front/side
stiles (4) $\frac{3}{4}$" x 3" x 34$\frac{1}{2}$"

H. Splines (2) $\frac{1}{4}$" x 1" x 34$\frac{1}{2}$"

J. Front rail $\frac{3}{4}$" x 3" x 19$\frac{7}{16}$"

K. Dowels (4) $\frac{3}{8}$" dia. x 2"

L. Door stiles (2) $\frac{3}{4}$" x 2$\frac{1}{2}$" x 31$\frac{3}{8}$"

M. Door rails (2) $\frac{3}{4}$" x 3" x 16$\frac{5}{16}$"

N. Door panel $\frac{1}{2}$" x 14$\frac{13}{16}$" x 26"

P. Pegs (4) $\frac{3}{8}$" x $\frac{3}{8}$" x 1$\frac{1}{4}$"*

Q. Door pull 1" x 1$\frac{1}{2}$" x 3"

R. Pivot $\frac{7}{16}$" dia. x 2$\frac{9}{16}$"

S. Latch $\frac{3}{4}$" x 1" x 3$\frac{1}{2}$"

T. Stop dowel $\frac{3}{8}$" dia. x 1$\frac{1}{4}$"

U. Shelving
support pins (4) $\frac{1}{4}$" dia. x 1"

*Trim the pegs to approximately $\frac{13}{16}$"
long after they are installed.*

HARDWARE

Hinges and mounting screws (1 pair)
#8 x 1$\frac{1}{4}$" Flathead wood screws
(20–24)

1

Select the stock and cut the parts to size. Country craftsmen used many different types of wood to build cupboards and cabinets. For a formal piece, they preferred walnut, cherry, and figured maple. For utilitarian furniture — or furniture that was painted — they used mostly pine and poplar. Since this cupboard was painted, it was built from pine.

To make the cupboard, you need approximately 30 board feet of 4/4 (four-quarters) lumber. Plane 3–4 board feet of stock ½″ thick (for the door panel) and the remainder ¾″ thick. You also need a scrap of 1″-thick stock (for the door pull), another scrap of ⅜″-thick stock (for the pegs), and several long scraps of ¼″ plywood (for the splines). The peg stock should be *very* hard — traditionally, old-time craftsmen used either rock maple or hickory for pegs.

When you have selected and planed the wood, glue up the stock needed for the top, bottom, shelves, back stiles, and door panel. Cut the parts to the sizes shown in the Materials List, except the door parts — you'll cut these later. Bevel the adjoining edges of the front and side stiles at 22½°, as shown in the *Top View*.

TRY THIS! You don't need to glue up stock that's 12″ wide along its entire length to make a back stile. Instead, glue boards together to make an L-shaped piece, as shown. This will save lumber.

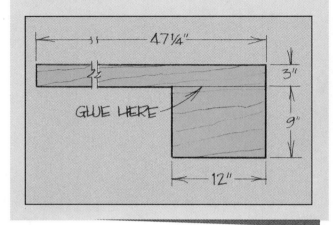

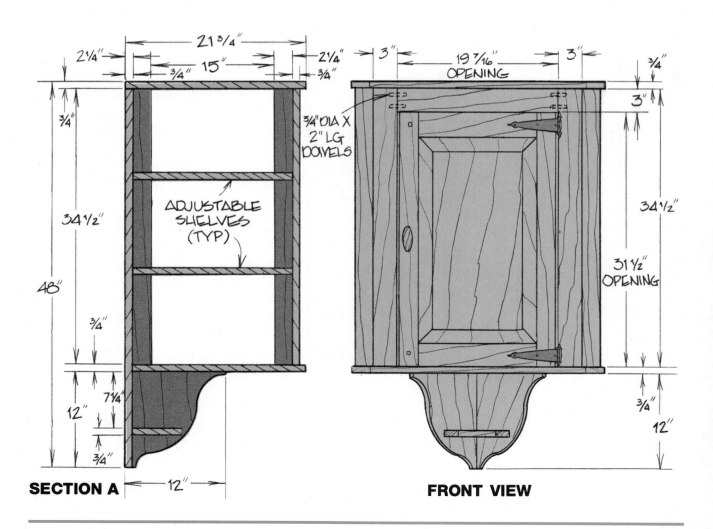

SECTION A

FRONT VIEW

2

Cut the shapes of the top, bottom, and shelves. Lay out the top, bottom, adjustable shelves, and scroll shelf. Cut the shapes, then sand or joint the sawed edges.

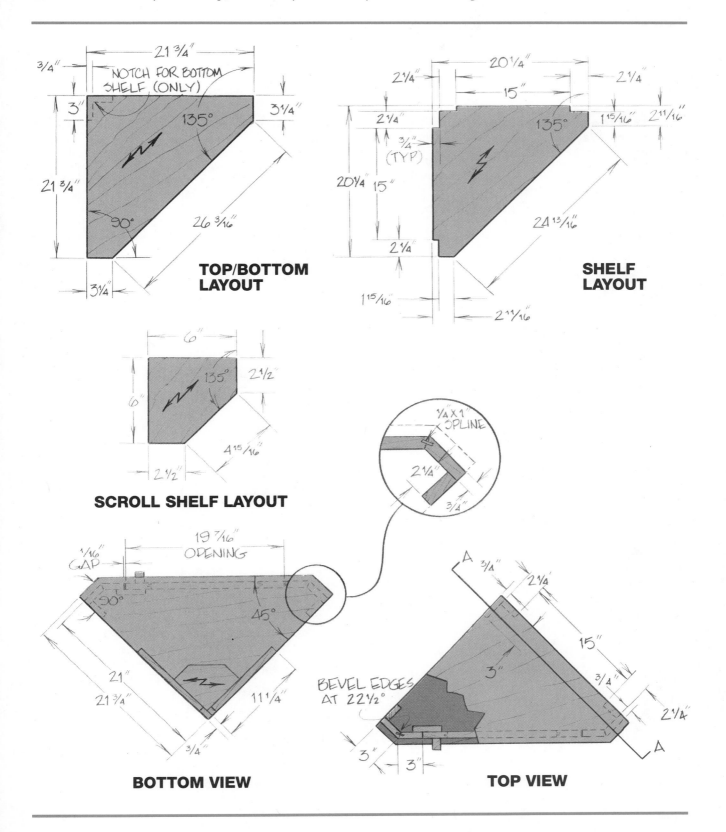

TOP/BOTTOM LAYOUT

SHELF LAYOUT

SCROLL SHELF LAYOUT

BOTTOM VIEW

TOP VIEW

3

Drill dowel holes in the front stiles and rail. The front rail joins the front stiles with dowels. Using a doweling jig, drill ³/₈″-diameter, 1″-deep dowel holes in the edges of the stiles and the ends of the rail.

Note: You can also use wooden plates or "biscuits" to join these parts, if you have a plate joiner. For extra strength, use two #20 plates in each joint.

4

Drill the shelving support holes and stop hole. Lay out the locations of the ¹/₄″-diameter holes on the inside faces of the side and back stiles, as shown on the *Side Stile Layout* and *Back Stile Layout*. Drill the holes ¹/₂″ deep. These will hold the pins that support the adjustable shelves.

Also, drill a ³/₈″-diameter, ¹/₂″-deep hole in the inside

face of the left front stile. This will hold the stop for the latch.

Note: The location of this hole will depend on where you plan to put the adjustable shelves. If you install a shelf too close to the stop and latch, it will interfere with the latch action. Give some thought to this before you drill the hole.

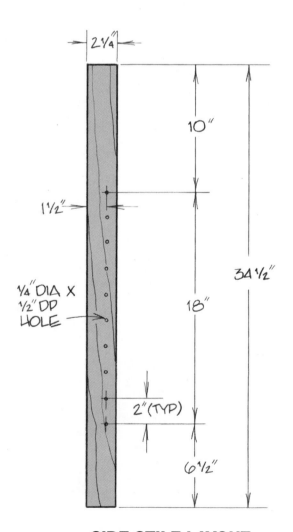

SIDE STILE LAYOUT

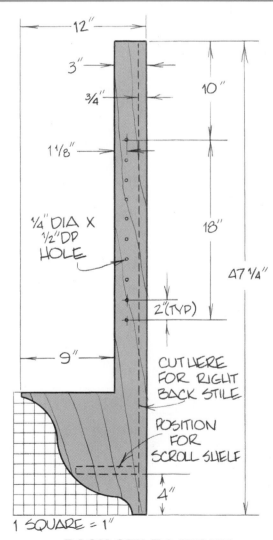

BACK STILE LAYOUT

5 Cut the shapes of the back stiles.

Enlarge the pattern shown in the *Back Stile* *Layout* and trace it on the stock. Cut the shapes with a band saw or saber saw, then sand the sawed edges.

6 Cut the spline grooves in the front and side stiles.

Mount a dado cutter accessory on the table saw, then tilt the cutter to 22½°. Using the fence as a guide, cut ¼″-wide, ½″-deep spline grooves in the beveled edges of the front and side stiles. (See Figure 1.)

1/Cut the spline grooves in the stiles with the cutter tilted to 22½°. You can also use an ordinary saw blade, but you'll have to make at least two passes to cut each groove ¼″ wide.

7 Assemble the case.

Finish sand the parts you have made so far, then assemble them as follows:

- Glue the back stiles together edge-to-face, forming a 90° corner.
- Glue the scroll shelf to the back stile, and reinforce it with flathead wood screws.
- Glue the front and side stiles together edge-to-edge, forming a 135° corner. Reinforce the edge joint with splines. (See Figure 2.)
- Glue the side and corner stiles together edge-to-face, forming a 90° corner.
- Glue and dowel the top rail between the two front stiles, end-to-edge.
- Using glue and flathead wood screws, assemble the top, bottom, back stile assembly, and front stile assembly.

You can drive some of the screws from the inside or back side of the case, so you won't see them when you have assembled the case. Countersink the screws, making the heads flush with the wood surface. When you attach the bottom and top, you'll have to drive these screws through the top or bottom into the stiles. Counterbore *and* countersink these "outside" screws, then cover the heads with wooden plugs. Sand the plugs flush with the wood surface.

2/When gluing parts with beveled edges together, use a simple "stop" jig. The two stops are strips of wood clamped to a plywood base. The strips hold the wooden parts in place, keeping them from collapsing or spreading before the glue sets. Several band clamps apply pressure to the joint.

TRY THIS! Old-time craftsmen used square-cut nails for assembly. If you wish to build an accurate reproduction of an antique, substitute hand forged or cut nails for the screws. Set the heads of the nails after you drive them.

8 Cut the parts for the door.

Measure the door opening on the assembled case — it may have changed slightly from what's shown on the draw- ings. If so, adjust the dimensions of the door parts as necessary and cut them to size.

9

Cut the door joinery. Use a dado cutter or table-mounted router to cut ¼"-wide, ⅜"-deep grooves in the inside edges of the door stiles and rails. Also cut ¼"-wide, 1"-long tenons on the ends of the rails. Using a band saw, notch these tenons as shown in the *Door Frame Assembly Detail*. These notches create a step or "haunch" in each tenon. (See Figures 3 through 5.)

To make the mortises, drill overlapping ¼"-diameter, 1"-deep holes in the stiles. Begin drilling ⅜" from the end of the stile. Make each series of holes 2⅛" long, and center it in the grooved edge of the stile. (Measure the depth of the holes from the edge of the stile — not the bottom of the groove.) Square the corners and clean up the mortises with a small chisel. The haunched tenons must fit snugly in the mortises so the outside edge of the rails is flush with the ends of the stiles. (See Figures 6 through 8.)

3/To make a "haunched" mortise-and-tenon joint, first cut grooves for the door panel in the inside edges of the adjoining rail and stile.

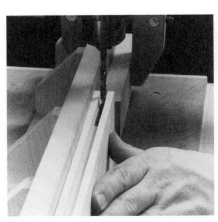

6/Cut the mortise for the haunched portion of the tenon by drilling a series of overlapping holes in the grooved edge of the stile. The holes should be as deep as the tenon is long.

4/Next, cut a tenon in the end of the rail. This tenon should be precisely the same width as the grooves, but much longer than the grooves are deep.

7/Clean up the mortise with a chisel, squaring the corners and trimming the sides flat.

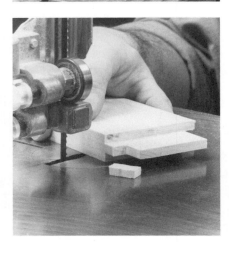

5/Using a band saw or a dovetail saw, cut a notch in the tenon, creating a step or "haunch." The haunch should be precisely as long as the grooves are deep.

8/The haunched tenon should be snug in the mortise (but not too tight). When assembled, the outside edge of the rail must be flush with the end of the stile.

10 **Raise the panel.** Using a table saw, bevel the ends and edges of the door panel at 15°, as shown on the *Door Section Detail*. This will "raise" the panel so it fits the grooves in the door frame.

TRY THIS! Use a hollow-ground planer blade, if you have one, to raise the panel. This blade leaves a very smooth cut, reducing the amount of sanding needed.

11 **Cut beads in the stiles.** With a router or molder, cut a 5/16″ bead in the outside face of each door stile, as shown in the *Door Section Detail*.

These beads — once called *cock beading* — were a popular decoration on eighteenth- and nineteenth-century door frames and drawer fronts.

12 **Assemble the door.** Finish sand the door parts, then glue the rails to the stiles. Place the door panel in the grooves as you assemble the frame, with the raised face out. Do *not* glue it to the rails or stiles; let it float in the grooves.

Whittle the pegs round along *most* of their length. Leave one end of each peg square, as shown in the *Peg Detail*. Drill a 3/8″-diameter hole through each mortise and tenon. Drive a peg, round end first, through this hole from the outside.

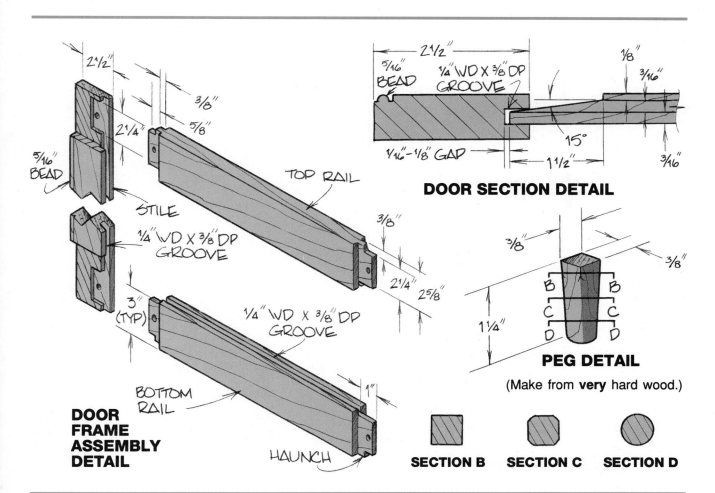

DOOR SECTION DETAIL

DOOR FRAME ASSEMBLY DETAIL

PEG DETAIL

(Make from **very** hard wood.)

SECTION B   SECTION C   SECTION D

Hammer the peg in until the square end is *almost* flush with the surface — leave about $1/16''$ protruding. Cut the round end of the peg flush with the back surface. (See Figure 9.)

This technique — driving a square peg into a round hole — was commonly used by country craftsmen to secure mortise-and-tenon joints. The pegs stay tight for dozens — perhaps hundreds — of years. But as the wood expands and contracts over many seasons, it pushes the pegs out of their holes a fraction of an inch. By letting the pegs on this new door protrude just above the wood surface, you simulate this natural process. This, in turn, makes the door frame appear older than it really is.

9/Let the square ends of the pegs protrude slightly on the outside of the door frame. This makes the project look aged.

13

Hang the door in the case. Fit the door to the case so there's about a $1/16''$ gap all around it. Mortise the right door stile and right front stile for hinges (if necessary), then attach the door to the case.

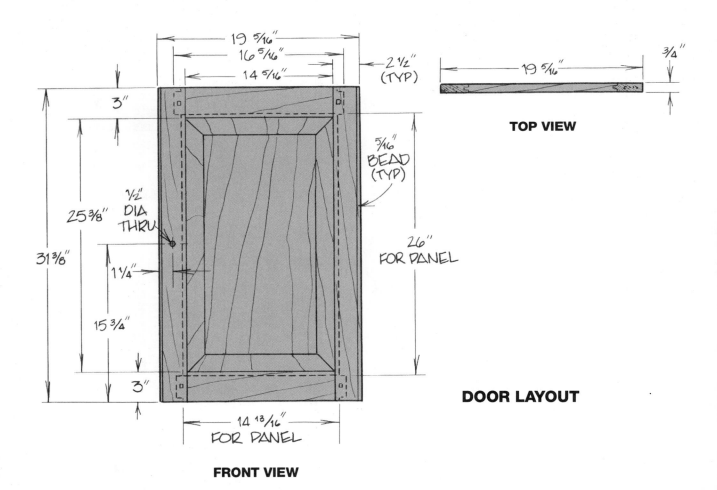

TOP VIEW

DOOR LAYOUT

FRONT VIEW

14

Install the pull and latch. Mark the position of the door pull and latch on the door. The pull should be centered in the left door stile, about ½" *above* the stop hole in the left front stile. Drill a ½"-diameter hole through the door frame at this point.

Drill a ⁷⁄₁₆"-diameter hole through the latch, as shown in the *Door Latch Assembly Detail,* and a ⁷⁄₁₆"-diameter, 1"-deep hole in the back face of the door pull stock, as shown in the *Door Pull Detail.* Using a band saw or a scroll saw, cut the shape of the door pull, then round the edges with a rasp and file.

Glue the pivot dowel in the door pull. Insert the dowel through the door, and glue the dowel in the latch. Turn the latch so it's perpendicular with the pull. Be careful not to get any glue on the door frame — the door pull assembly should turn easily. Finally, glue the stop dowel in the inside face of the front stile.

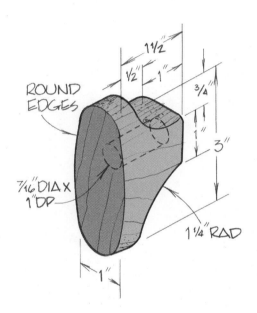

DOOR LATCH ASSEMBLY DETAIL

DOOR PULL DETAIL

15

Finish the cupboard. Remove the door from the cupboard and the hinges from the door. With a rasp or file, round over the edges of the cupboard and door to make the piece look old and worn. Do any necessary touch-up sanding, but be careful not to sand the pegs flush with the door frame. Apply a finish to the completed project, then replace the door on the cupboard.

If you hang the cupboard from a frame wall, use long wood screws. Drive these screws through the *back* stiles. Since most homes are built with studs where the walls meet (at the corners of the rooms), the screws should bite into solid wood. If you hang the cupboard from a masonry wall, use expandable lead anchors instead of screws.

Step-by-Step: Grain Painting

During the late eighteenth and early nineteenth centuries, big-city craftsmen began to cover their furniture with highly figured, exotic veneers. Country craftsmen and their clients couldn't often afford these veneers —the veneer had to be imported over long distances — so they developed methods of painting a piece to look veneered. They called this *grain painting*.

1

To grain-paint a project, first apply the base color. This can be latex, enamel, colored lacquer — almost any type of paint. If you want to produce a realistic imitation of wood, this base coat should be a natural wood tone. However, country "grainers" used all colors.

2

Seal the base color with a clear, fast-drying finish, such as shellac or lacquer. This will prevent the base coat from soaking up too much of the grain color.

5

While the grain color is still wet, drag the graining tool through it. This will expose some of the base color, creating patterns and textures. Make zigzags to imitate curly grain, round dots for bird's-eyes and blisters, swirled shapes for burls. There are no rules; you can do anything that looks good to you.

6

For different effects, you can apply the grain color with the graining tool, instead of dragging the tool through the wet color. "Grainers" often use a stiff brush or a sponge as an applicator.

Grain painting is a simple technique — cover one color of paint with another, then texture the second color. However, you can produce many delightful effects. With a bit of practice, you can make the paint look like a primitive imitation of veneer. This will give your project a rustic charm. Or, with a little more practice, you can make it look almost exactly like an expensive veneer.

Use artist's oils for the grain color. Choose a color that contrasts sharply with the base color. Put a little dab of paint on the edge of a dish and fill the dish with linseed oil. Dip a brush in the oil, then in the color. Depending on the effect you want, mix the color and the oil to a thick, opaque coat or a thin, transparent wash. Paint the mixture over the base color.

Use a graining tool to texture the grain color. This tool can be almost anything — a stiff brush, crumpled newspaper, a sponge, a lump of clay or glazing putty, corrugated cardboard, a commercial tool from a craft supply store, even your fingers. You may also use more than one tool for different effects. Only experimentation will tell you which one does which.

After texturing, let the grain color dry completely. Then apply another coat of clear finish to protect it.

If you wish, you can repeat the last few steps, applying several layers of grain colors. (If you're after a realistic wood grain, this will produce better results.) Let each layer dry completely and cover it with a clear finish before applying the next.

Spoon and Plate Rack

F amilies once kept all their dinnerware on racks like this — plates, bowls, cups, and utensils. To save space, they stood the plates and bowls on edge toward the backs of the shelves, and placed the cups in front or dangled them from hooks underneath. Spoons and forks hung from the front edges of the shelves. These utensils created a fence of sorts that helped prevent the plates, bowls, and cups from slipping off the shelves.

Today, most families couldn't fit their dinner service on a small rack. But the old racks are still useful. They make good places to display collections of small items — keepsakes, boxes, dolls, old tools, and (of course) plates and spoons.

The rack shown is a hanging set of narrow shelves with cove and bead molding around the top. Each shelf has a groove to hold the rims of plates, and several dovetail-shaped notches to hold spoons. A rail above each shelf keeps the plates upright, in case the rack accidentally should be pulled out from the wall. These rails are also used to mount the rack to the wall.

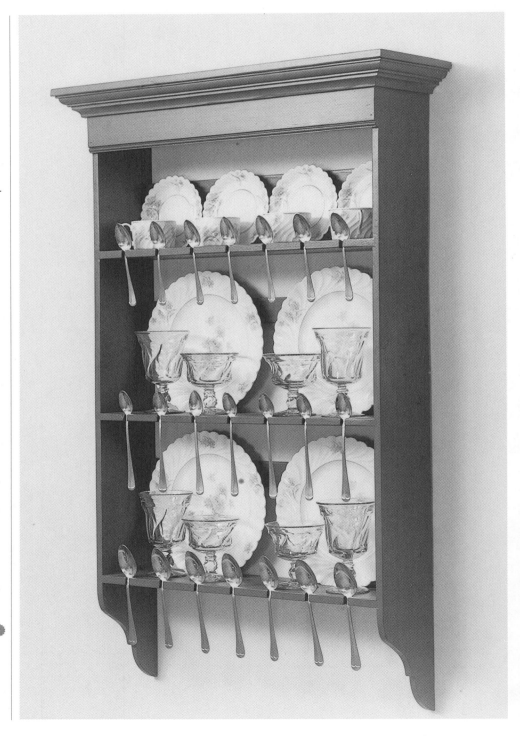

L. L. Johnson Lumber Mfg. Co.

P.O. BOX 278, 563 N. COCHRAN STREET
CHARLOTTE, MICHIGAN 48813
Federal I.D. #38-1801302

REMIT TO: JOHNSON'S WORKBENCH

☐ 563 N. COCHRAN, CHARLOTTE, MI 48813
(517) 543-2727 FAX (517) 543-7180
Sales Tax #ME01-02-646

☐ 51315 N. US-33, SOUTH BEND, IN 46637
(219) 277-8350 FAX (219) 272-8798
Sales Tax #381801302016

Everything For The Woodworker!
JOHNSON'S
WORKBENCH

Charlotte   South Bend

INVOICE NUMBER	DATE
411202	13.06.37 SEP/13/91

PURCHASE ORDER NO.	SOLD BY
	EV

SOLD TO WOOD, WIDGETS, & WHIRLIGI

PRODUCT CODE	PART NUMBER	DESCRIPTION	QUANTITY SOLD	UNIT PRICE	TOTAL PRICE
130	103001	1/4 X 36 OAK	4	0.40	1.60
# 120	061038	3/8 R OAK	4	7.98	7.98
# 120	061001	1/4 RED OAK	1	1.27	1.27
				SUBTOTAL	10.85
				TAX	0.00
				TOTAL	10.85

TERMS:

James E. Pickett (signature)

ALL CLAIMS AND GOODS **MUST**
BE ACCOMPANIED BY THIS BILL

Thank You!

CUSTOMER COPY

Materials List

FINISHED DIMENSIONS

PARTS

A. Sides (2) $1/2'' \times 5^3/4'' \times 41^3/4''$

B. Shelves (3) $1/2'' \times 5^3/4'' \times 23''$

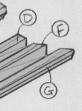

C. Rails (3) $1/2'' \times 1^3/4'' \times 23^1/2''$

D. Valance $1/2'' \times 4'' \times 23^1/2''$

E. Top $1/2'' \times 7^1/2'' \times 27''$

F. Cove molding (total) $3/4'' \times 1^1/2'' \times 40''$

G. Bead molding $3/4'' \times 3/4'' \times 43''$

EXPLODED VIEW

HARDWARE

#8 x 1¼" Flathead wood screws (10)

#8 x 1¼" Roundhead wood screws and flat washers (2)

1" Wire brads (8–12)

³/₈"-diameter Wooden plugs (4–6)

#10 x 2½" Roundhead wood screws (2–4), or ¼" Molly anchors and bolts (2–4)

1

Select the stock and cut the parts to size. Ordinarily, plate racks were made from whatever wood was on hand, then covered with milk paint. Since the paint concealed the wood, the species didn't matter. Country craftsmen mostly used white pine, but plate racks might also be made from poplar, cherry, walnut, ash — almost any domestic wood.

Whatever stock you choose, you'll need about 14 board feet of 4/4 (four-quarters, or 1″-thick) lumber to make this project.

Plane the stock to the thicknesses needed — 3/4″ for the moldings and 1/2″ for the remainder of the parts. Cut the parts to size, except the moldings. Cut these 1/2″ to 1″ wider than specified in the Materials List.

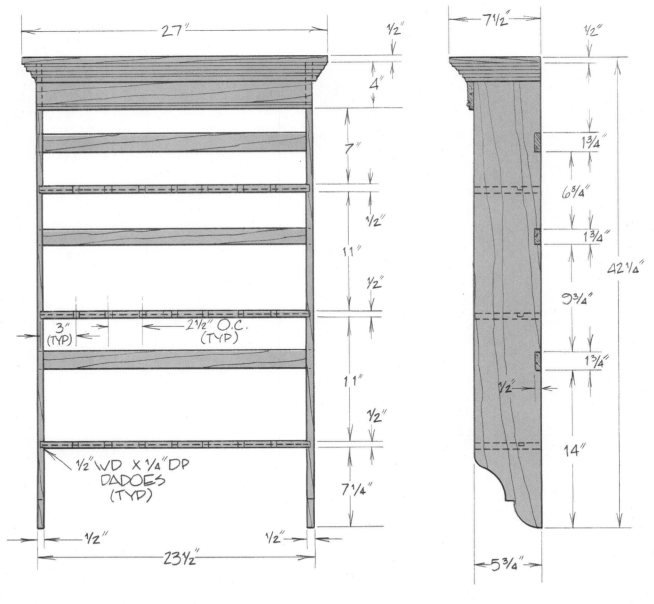

FRONT VIEW   **SIDE VIEW**

2 Cut the dadoes and grooves.

As shown in the *Front View,* the shelves are spaced 11″ apart. (The standard diameter of a dinner plate is 10″.) Depending on what you want to put on these shelves, you may want to adjust the spacing. When you have decided where to place the shelves, cut ½″-wide, ¼″-deep dadoes in the sides to hold them, using a dado cutter or a router.

Also cut ¼″-wide, ¼″-deep grooves in the top faces of the shelves. Place these grooves 1½″ from the back edge, as shown in the *Plate Groove Detail.* As men-

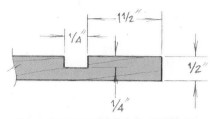

PLATE GROOVE DETAIL

tioned, the grooves hold the rims of the plates. If you don't plan to display plates on the shelves, you may want to eliminate the grooves.

3 Cut the shapes and the notches in the sides.

Stack the side pieces face to face, with the dadoes in one piece facing the dadoes in the other. Tape the pieces together, making sure the dadoes line up. Enlarge the *Side Pattern* and trace it on the top piece, and measure and mark the notches along the back edge. These notches hold the rails. Remember, if you've changed the positions of the shelves, you'll have to adjust the position of the notches to correspond.

Cut the side pattern and the notches with a band saw or saber saw. Sand the sawed edges of the pattern to remove the saw marks. To fit the rails snugly in the notches, cut just inside the lines, then enlarge each notch with a rasp or file until the rail slips into place.

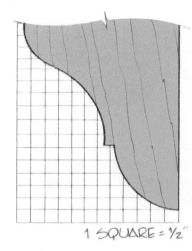

1 SQUARE = ½″

SIDE PATTERN

4 Cut the dovetail notches in the shelves.

Stack the shelves with the plate grooves all facing in the same direction. Tape the stack together, then measure and mark the positions of the dovetail notches in the front edges of the shelves. As shown in the *Front View* and the *Dovetail Notch Detail,* these notches are spaced 3″ on center. You may space them closer together, if you have more than 21 spoons to display. If you don't plan to display spoons, you may want to eliminate the notches.

Cut the notches using a table-mounted router and a dovetail bit. Set the bit ³⁄₈″ above the table. Line up the first mark on the shelves with the bit. Using a miter gauge as a guide, pass the entire stack of shelves over the bit. (See Figure 1.) Line up the second mark and repeat. Continue until you have cut all the notches in all three shelves.

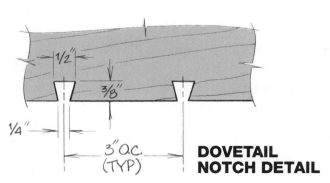

DOVETAIL NOTCH DETAIL

1/Rout the dovetail notches in the front edges of the shelves with a table-mounted router. Back up the cuts with a scrap so the bit doesn't tear or chip the wood as it exits.

5 **Cut the bead in the valance.** Cut a bead in the edge of the valance, as shown in the *Front Molding Detail.* You can make this shape using a molder accessory on a table saw, or a table-mounted router. If you use a molder, mount three-bead knives in the molding head. Adjust the position of the fence over the molder so you will cut only a single ³⁄₁₆″-diameter bead near the edge of the valance. (See Figure 2.)

If you use a router, mount a point-cut quarter-round bit in the chuck. Set the bit just slightly above the table. Cut the bead in two passes, using a fence to guide the valance stock. (See Figure 3.)

Note: Since these bits normally cut a ¼″-diameter bead, the profile will not be exactly as it appears in the drawings.

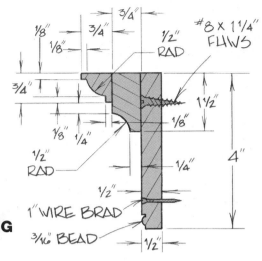

FRONT MOLDING DETAIL

2/If you use a molder to make the bead, cover the unused portion of the knives with the fence. Cut a hollow or a notch in the fence, as shown, to fit over the molder. This will make the setup much safer.

3/To use a table-mounted router to make the bead, mount a **point-cut quarter-round** bit in the chuck, and cut the bead in two passes. Move the fence slightly for the second pass.

6 **Assemble the shelving unit.** Finish sand the sides, shelves, valance, top, and rails. Then glue the sides, shelves, and rails together, setting the top and valance aside for the moment. Check that the assembly is square as you clamp it up.

Let the glue cure, then reinforce the glue joints. At the back of the assembly, drive flathead wood screws through the rails and into the sides. Countersink the screws. Near the front, drive wire brads at an angle, up through the shelves and into the sides. (See Figure 4.) If you should have trouble starting the brads, drill ¹⁄₁₆″-diameter pilot holes, about ¼″ deep. Drive the brads as far as you can without marring the wood, then use a nail set to drive them the rest of the way and set the heads.

Glue the valance to the sides, then reinforce it with screws *and* brads. Drive the screws near the top edge of the valance, countersinking the heads. (When you attach the molding to the project, you'll cover the screws.) Drive the brads near the bottom edge of the valance, and set the heads.

Sand the outside faces of the sides, making the ends of the rails and the valance clean and flush. Attach the top to the assembly with glue and screws. Counterbore and countersink the screws, then glue wooden plugs in the counterbores to hide the screw heads.

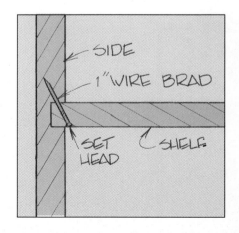

4/To reinforce the dado joints, drive wire brads into the underside of each shelf. Angle the brads so they go up through the shelf and into the side. After you set the heads, they won't be noticeable.

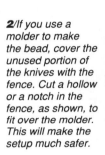

7
Make the molding. Using a router or a shaper, cut a ½″-radius cove in one edge of the cove molding stock. Cut a *stepped* ½″-radius bead in the bead stock, as shown in the *Front Molding Detail*. Glue the two pieces together, face to face, with the bead molding on top of the cove molding. The bottom edges should be parallel and ¾″ apart. Let the glue dry, then rip the assembled moldings 1½″ wide. (See Figure 5.)

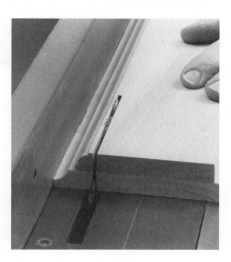

5/After gluing them together, rip the moldings on a table saw. **Saw-guard removed for clarity.**

8
Attach the moldings. Carefully measure the width and depth of the shelf assembly. With all the sanding, it's likely that the dimensions will have changed slightly from those given in the drawings. Cut the front and side moldings to fit the rack, mitering the adjoining ends.

Attach the front molding first, gluing it to the valance and the top. To attach the side moldings, first drill a ¼″-diameter hole through each side, near the back top corner and no more than ¾″ from the top edge. Glue the side moldings to the front moldings and the valance, *but don't glue them to the sides or the top.* Instead, drive #8 x 1¼″ roundhead wood screws with washers through the holes and into the moldings, as shown in the *Side Molding Detail*.

Note: The screws and the oversized holes are necessary because the grain of the sides and top runs perpendicular to the moldings. If you glue the moldings in

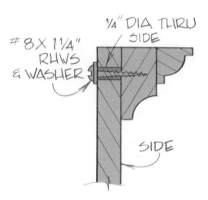

SIDE MOLDING DETAIL

place, the top or the sides will buckle as they expand and contract. Instead, the screws move back and forth in the holes, letting the parts move without distorting.

9
Finish and hang the plate rack. Do any necessary touch-up sanding on the plate rack, then apply paint or a finish. When the finish dries, hang the rack on a wall. If you can center the rack over one or more studs, drive #10 x 2½″ roundhead wood

screws through the rails and into the studs. To attach it to a hollow wall between studs, install Molly anchors in the wall. Then drive roundhead bolts through the rails and into the Molly anchors.

Low Shelves

Like all country furniture, shelves were designed to make the most efficient use of the available space. Shelving units usually either stood floor-to-ceiling, or they hung on a wall above another piece of furniture. Short, standing shelves like those shown here were less common. Country folks, however, sometimes made them if there was a need.

These low shelves were useful in attic rooms, where the side walls were only three or four feet high. Storekeepers sometimes displayed goods on shelves like these, and used the tops as counters. Or the shelves might sit in a hallway, beneath a picture or a mirror.

Since they were not a common piece, they have no real name. An eighteenth- or nineteenth-century gentleman might list them in his inventory simply as a "short rack" or "low shelves."

Materials List

FINISHED DIMENSIONS

PARTS

A. Sides (2) $3/4'' \times 9^3/4'' \times 36^3/4''$
B. Top $3/4'' \times 11^1/4'' \times 38''$
C. Shelves (3) $3/4'' \times 9^3/4'' \times 35^3/4''$
D. Stiles (2) $3/4'' \times 2^1/4'' \times 36^3/4''$
E. Rails (2) $3/4'' \times 3'' \times 32''$
F. Dowels (12) $3/8''$ dia. $\times 2''$

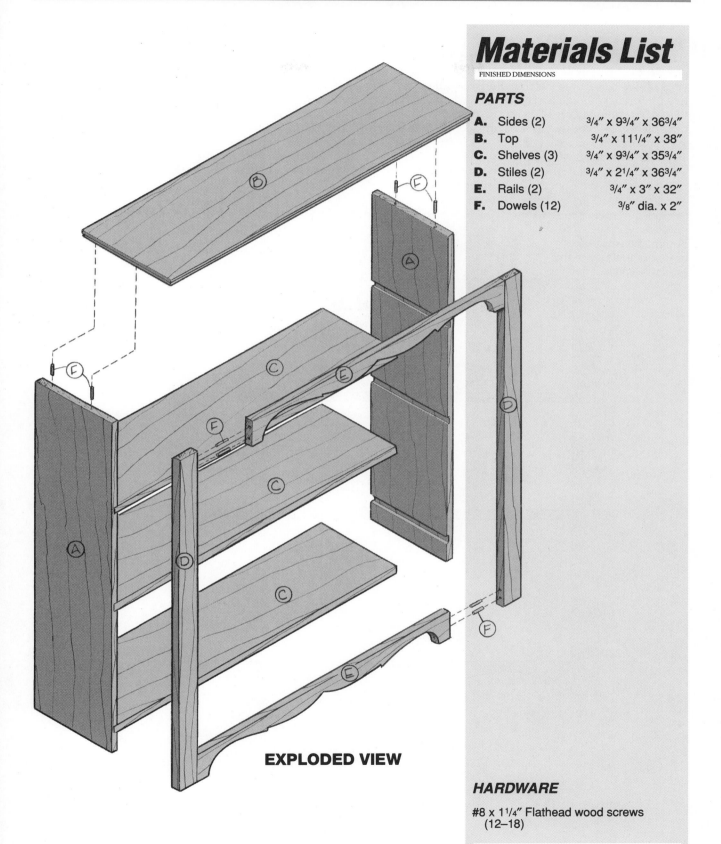

EXPLODED VIEW

HARDWARE

#8 x 1¹/₄″ Flathead wood screws
(12–18)

1

Select the materials and cut the parts to size. Country craftsmen used many different types of wood to make shelving. For a formal piece, they preferred walnut, cherry, and figured maple. For utilitarian furniture, they used mostly pine and poplar. If the piece was expected to see hard service, they used oak, hickory, rock maple, or birch. The shelving unit shown is made from white pine.

You can easily adjust the height, width, or depth of the piece to suit your needs by changing the corre-

sponding measurements of the parts. For example, if you need wider shelves, make the top, shelves, and rails longer. If you want to build a taller unit, stretch the sides and stiles.

The shelves shown in the drawings require approximately 20 board feet of lumber. If you change the size, however, the amount of material needed will change also. When you have determined the type and the amount of wood needed, cut the parts to size.

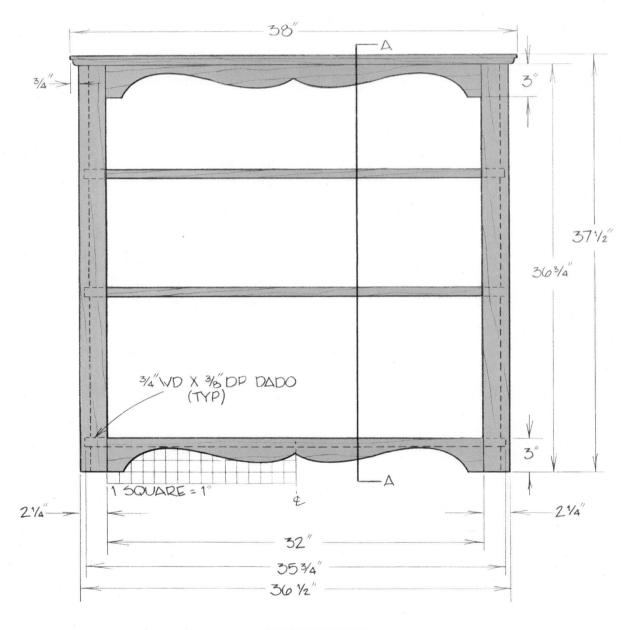

FRONT VIEW

2 Cut the dadoes in the sides.
The shelves in this unit are all "fixed" — held permanently in dadoes. Rout or cut these dadoes in the sides, as shown in *Section A*.

TRY THIS! If you wish, make the middle shelves adjustable. Instead of cutting dadoes, drill two rows of $\frac{1}{4}$"-diameter, $\frac{1}{2}$"-deep holes in each side, as shown in the *Alternate Side Layout*. After you complete the shelves, insert pin-style supports in these holes to hold the shelves.

3 Shape the top edge.
Using a router or shaper, shape the front edge and both ends of the top. (Do *not* shape the back edge.) You may use the ogee shape shown in the *Top Edge Profile,* or any other shape that suits your fancy.

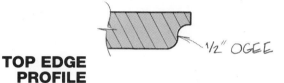

TOP EDGE PROFILE

$\frac{1}{2}$" OGEE

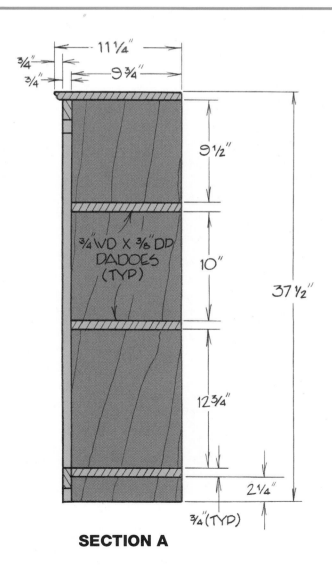

SECTION A

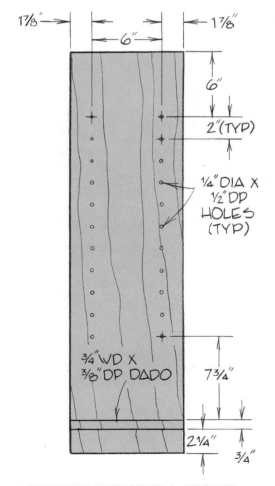

ALTERNATE SIDE LAYOUT

4 Drill the dowel holes in the rails and stiles.
As shown, the front frame is doweled together, with two dowels in each joint. Using a dowel-ing jig, drill ³⁄₈"-diameter, 1"-deep dowel holes in the ends of the rails and edges of the stiles.

TRY THIS! If you have a plate joiner, you can also use wooden plates or "biscuits" to join the rails and stiles. Use two plates per joint, as shown.

5 Cut the shapes of the rails.
Stack the rails on top of each other and tape them together. Lay out the shape of the rails, as shown in the *Front View,* on the stock. Cut both rails at once, using a band saw or saber saw. With the parts still stacked together, sand the sawed edges. Remove the tape.

To get a strong bond, wipe the surface of the boards with a tack cloth *before* applying the tape.

TRY THIS! Use double-sided carpet tape to hold parts together for pad-sawing, pad-sanding, and similar operations. This keeps the boards from shifting better than ordinary masking tape.

6 Assemble the parts.
Finish sand the sides, shelves, and top. Dry assemble all the parts — including the rails and stiles — to test the fit of the joints. Adjust the fit as necessary.

Assemble the face frame with glue and make sure it is square. Set it aside to dry. Assemble the sides and shelves with glue and flathead screws, driving the screws up through the shelves and into the sides at an angle, as shown in the *Shelf-To-Side Joinery Detail.* Make sure that the assembly is square. If not, adjust it before the glue sets.

When the glue dries, sand all the joints clean and flush. Finish sand the face frame, and glue it to the front edges of the sides.

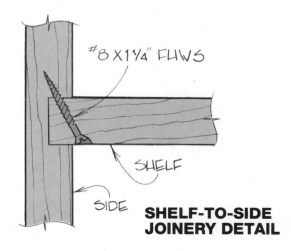

#8 X 1¼" FHWS

SHELF

SIDE

SHELF-TO-SIDE JOINERY DETAIL

Drill ³⁄₈″-diameter, 1½″-deep dowel holes in the top ends of the sides, as shown in the *Assembly Detail*. Place dowel centers in these holes, then position the top over the centers. Press the top down firmly, so the dowel centers leave small indentations in the bottom face of the top. At each of these indentations, drill ³⁄₈″-diameter, ½″-deep dowel holes. Then attach the top to the shelving assembly with dowels and glue.

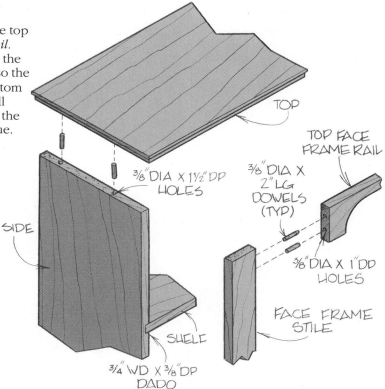

ASSEMBLY DETAIL

TOP

TOP FACE FRAME RAIL

³⁄₈″ DIA × 1½″ DP HOLES

³⁄₈″ DIA × 2″ LG DOWELS (TYP)

SIDE

³⁄₈″ DIA × 1″ DP HOLES

FACE FRAME STILE

SHELF

³⁄₄″ WD × ³⁄₈″ DP DADO

TRY THIS! You must drive the screws that hold the shelves to the sides at just the right angle. If the angle is too steep or too shallow, the end of the screw may show. To help install the screws correctly, make a drill guide from hardwood. The guide should have *two* angled holes — a large hole for the counterbore, and a smaller one for the pilot. Drill each hole in two steps — first the counterbore, then the pilot. Use stop collars on the bits to control the depth of the holes.

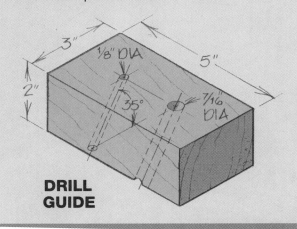

3″ ⅛″ DIA 5″

2″ 35° ⁷⁄₁₆″ DIA

DRILL GUIDE

7 **Finish the completed shelves.** Do any necessary touch-up sanding to the shelves, then apply a finish. To help prevent the project from warping or distorting, apply the finish evenly to *all* the wooden surfaces — inside and outside, top and bottom.

Sawtooth Shelves

Country cabinet-makers sometimes made shelving projects in which the shelves could be taken out, added, or rearranged. However, they didn't have the benefit of all the adjustable shelving hardware we have today — standards, brackets, pins, and clips. They devised their own systems, and built them from wood.

One popular old-time design was this sawtooth system, made from strips of wood in which the cabinetmaker cut triangular teeth. He mounted four sawtooth standards inside the case, two to a side. The teeth of each pair of standards faced each other. He placed short, narrow boards with pointed ends between these — the points fit snugly between the teeth. The shelves rested on these supports.

The unit shown was made to fit a wall in a small country home. It has three bays, and each bay has a set of sawtooth standards. You may build the unit as shown, add to or reduce the number of bays, or make each bay a separate unit.

EXPLODED VIEW

Materials List

FINISHED DIMENSIONS

PARTS

For Three Bays

A.	End stiles (6)	$3/4''$ x $2''$ x $71\frac{1}{4}''$
B.	Top/middle end rails (4)	$3/4''$ x $2''$ x $10''$
C.	Bottom end rails (2)	$3/4''$ x $3\frac{3}{4}''$ x $10''$
D.	End panels (4)	$1/2''$ x $9\frac{3}{4}''$ x $32\frac{3}{8}''$
E.	Middle front stiles (2)	$3/4''$ x $2''$ x $67\frac{1}{2}''$
F.	Top front rail	$3/4''$ x $2''$ x $85''$
G.	Bottom front rail	$3/4''$ x $3''$ x $85''$
H.	Right/left back stiles (2)	$3/4''$ x $2\frac{5}{8}''$ x $68\frac{1}{4}''$
J.	Long back stiles (4)	$3/4''$ x $2''$ x $68\frac{1}{4}''$
K.	Short back stiles (3)	$3/4''$ x $2''$ x $64\frac{1}{4}''$
L.	Top back rails (3)	$3/4''$ x $2''$ x $25\frac{3}{4}''$
M.	Bottom back rails (3)	$3/4''$ x $2\frac{3}{4}''$ x $25\frac{3}{4}''$
N.	Back panels (6)	$1/4''$ x $12\frac{1}{4}''$ x $64\frac{1}{4}''$
P.	Top	$3/4''$ x $14\frac{3}{4}''$ x $90\frac{1}{2}''$
Q.	Bottom shelf	$3/4''$ x $14''$ x $87\frac{1}{2}''$
R.	Cleats (2)	$3/4''$ x $3/4''$ x $13\frac{1}{4}''$
S.	Dividers (2)	$3/4''$ x $12\frac{1}{2}''$ x $67\frac{1}{2}''$
T.	Sawtooth strips (12)	$1/2''$ x $1''$ x $67\frac{1}{2}''$
U.	Shelf supports (24–30)	$1/2''$ x $1''$ x $11\frac{1}{2}''$
V.	Right/left adjustable shelves (8–10)	$3/4''$ x $12\frac{1}{2}''$ x $28\frac{7}{8}''$
W.	Middle adjustable shelves (4–5)	$3/4''$ x $12\frac{1}{2}''$ x $28\frac{1}{4}''$

HARDWARE

4d Finishing nails ($1/4$ lb.)
$7/8''$ Wire brads (1 box)
#10 x $1\frac{1}{4}''$ Flathead wood screws (18–24)

1

Select the stock and cut the parts to size. To build this project as shown, you'll need about 120 board feet of 4/4 (four-quarters) lumber and two 4' x 8' sheets of ¼″ cabinet-grade plywood. This shelving unit is made from oak and oak-veneer plywood, but you can use almost any type of cabinet-grade lumber. Walnut, cherry, maple, pine, poplar, oak, and ash were the most common for projects like these.

After choosing the lumber, plane about 20 board feet to ½″ thick, and the remainder to ¾″. Cut all the parts to the sizes shown in the Materials List, except the adjustable shelves, shelf supports, and sawtooth strips. Wait to fit these to the assembled case.

TRY THIS! On large projects, it is extremely important that the wood be as stable as possible *before* you work with it. There will be a difference in humidity between the lumberyard and your shop, and this will cause the boards to expand or contract after you bring them home. If you begin woodworking right away, the parts may change dimensions between the time you cut them and the time you assemble them. To prevent this, stack the wood in your shop and let it sit for *at least* a month.

2

Cut the tongues and grooves. This shelving unit is made of frames and panels, largely assembled with tongue-and-groove joints. Using a dado cutter or a table-mounted router, cut ¼″-wide, ⅜″-deep grooves in all the inside edges of the end stiles, right and left back stiles, long back stiles, top end rails, bottom end rails, top back rails, and bottom back rails. Cut grooves in *both* edges of the end middle rails and short back stiles.

Using the same tool, cut ¼″-thick, ⅜″-long tongues in the ends of all the rails. These tongues should be snug — but not too tight — in the grooves.

3

Cut rabbets in the back end stiles. The right and left back assemblies rest in ¾″-wide, ⅜″-deep rabbets in the back end stiles, as shown in the *Case Joinery Detail.* Cut these rabbets, using a dado cutter or table-mounted router.

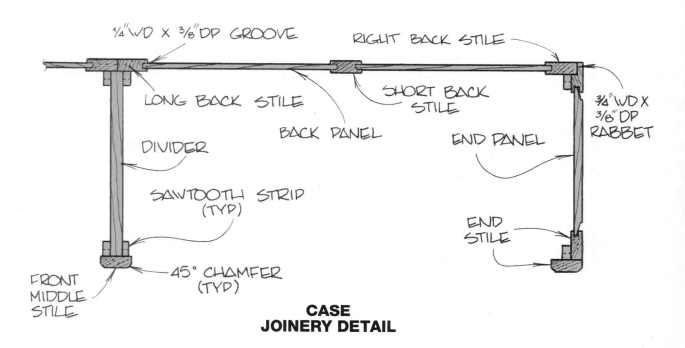

**CASE
JOINERY DETAIL**

4 **_Raise the end panels._** Using a table saw and a hollow-ground planer blade, raise the outside face of the end panels. (See Figure 1.) The beveled edges and ends of the panels must fit loosely in the rail and stile grooves, as shown in *Section B*.

1/To raise a panel on a table saw, tilt the blade to 15°. Adjust the fence and the blade height so the blade will cut a bevel with a small "step," as shown in **Section B.** Cut both edges and both ends of each panel.

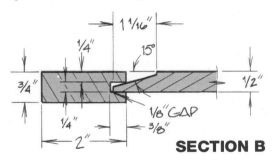

SECTION B

5 **_Assemble the panels._** Finish sand all the rails, stiles, and panels. Then assemble the ends and backs, gluing the rail tenons in the stile grooves. Work from top to bottom, sliding the panels into the grooves in the rails and stiles as you go. Do *not* glue the panels in place. Let them float in the grooves. Make certain that all these assemblies are square as you clamp them up. Otherwise, they won't fit together properly. When the glue dries, sand all joints clean and flush.

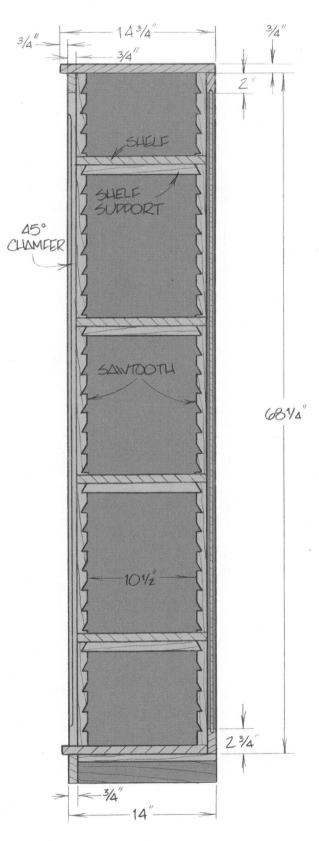

SECTION A

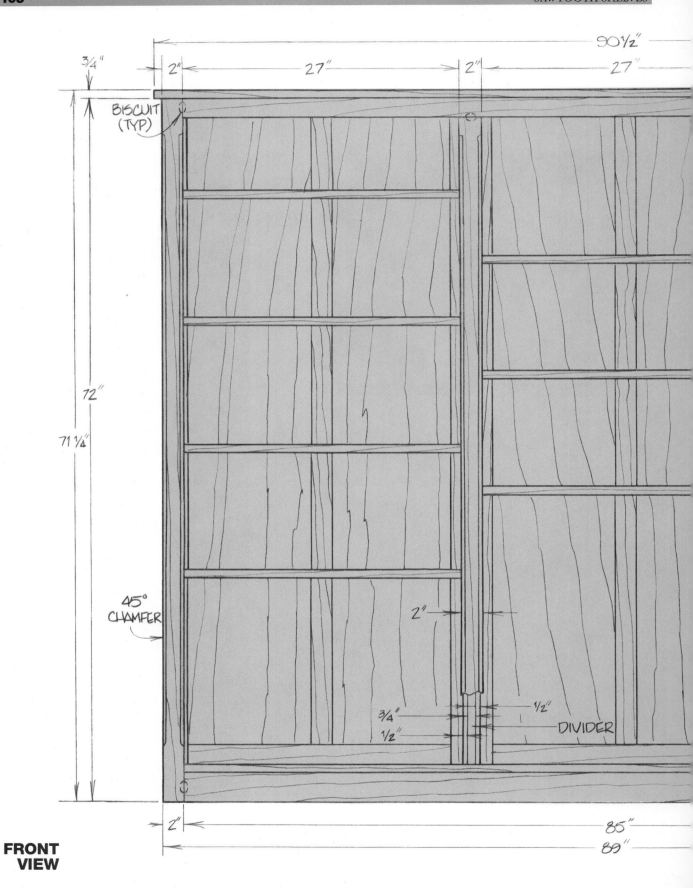

FRONT
VIEW

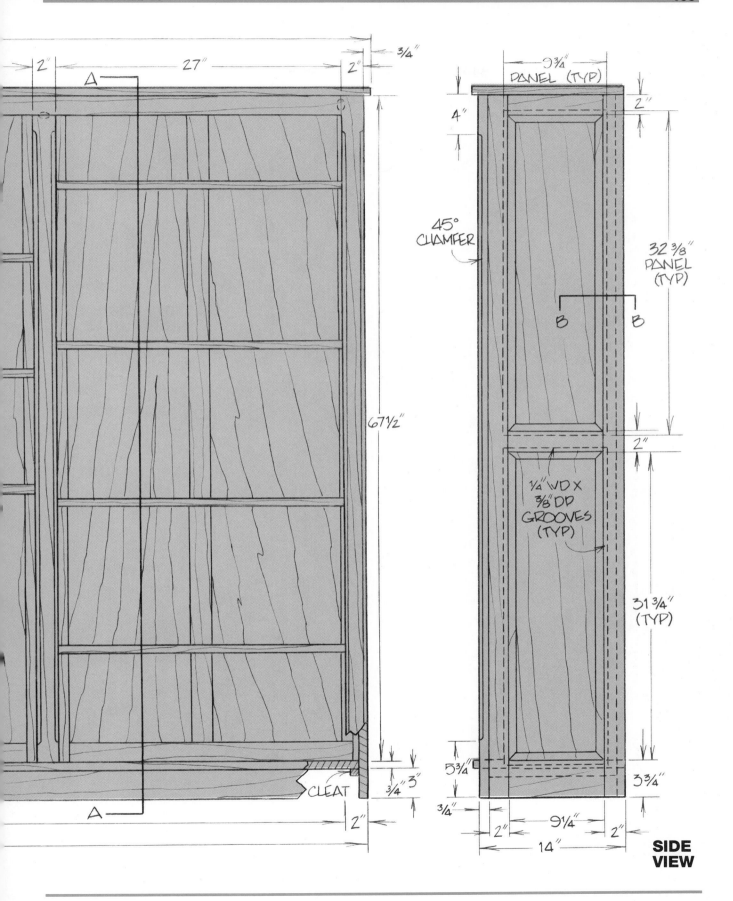

2"
27"
3/4"
2"
A
67½"
CLEAT
3/4" 3"
A
2"

9¾"
PANEL (TYP)
4"
2"
45°
CHAMFER
32 ⅜"
PANEL
(TYP)
B   B
2"
¼" WD X
⅜" DD
GROOVES
(TYP)
31¾"
(TYP)
5¾"
3¾"
3/4"
2"   9¼"   2"
14"

SIDE VIEW

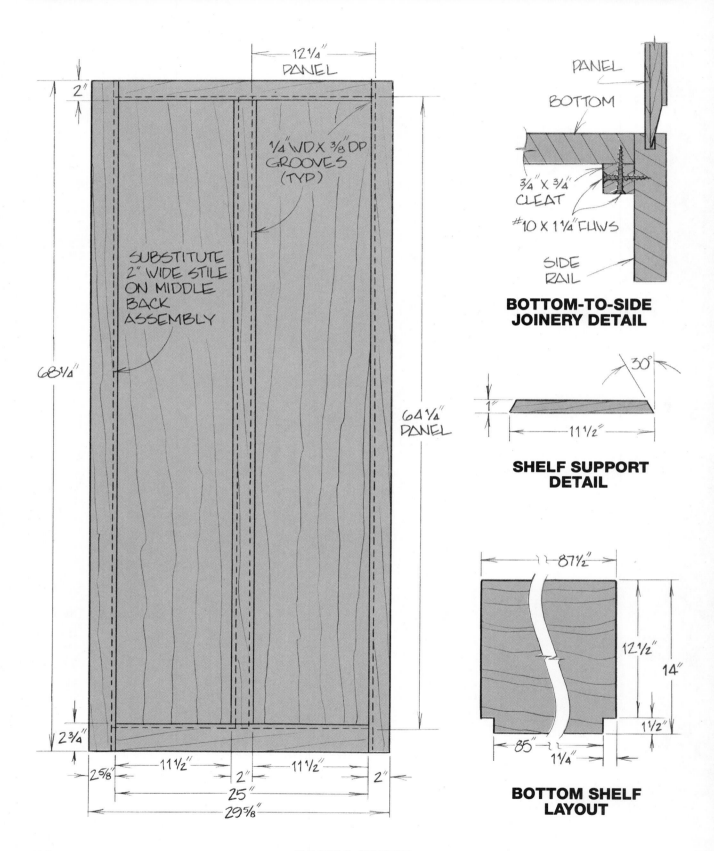

12¼"
PANEL

2"

¼" WD X ⅜" DP
GROOVES
(TYP)

SUBSTITUTE
2" WIDE STILE
ON MIDDLE
BACK
ASSEMBLY

68¼"

64¼"
PANEL

2¾"

2⅝"   11½"   2"   11½"   2"

25"

29⅝"

BACK LAYOUT

PANEL

BOTTOM

¾" X ¾"
CLEAT

#10 X 1¼" FHWS

SIDE
RAIL

**BOTTOM-TO-SIDE
JOINERY DETAIL**

30°

1"

11½"

**SHELF SUPPORT
DETAIL**

87½"

12½"

14"

1½"

85"

1¼"

**BOTTOM SHELF
LAYOUT**

6

Cut notches in the bottom shelf. The bottom shelf is notched to fit around the right and left front end stiles. Cut these notches with a saber saw, as shown in the *Bottom Shelf Layout.*

7

Assemble the case. Finish sand the top, bottom shelf, and dividers. Carefully measure and mark the top and bottom shelf where you will attach the dividers. Dry assemble the parts to check that they fit properly. Then assemble the case parts in this order:

- Attach the cleats to the ends with glue and flathead wood screws. Countersink the screws so the heads are flush with the surface.
- Assemble the top, bottom shelf, and end assemblies with screws and nails. Do *not* glue them together. You'll find it easier to put these parts together while they're horizontal, resting on their front edges. Drive screws through the cleats and into the bottom shelf, countersinking the screws. Tack the top in place with finishing nails. Let the heads of the nails protrude, so you can remove them later.

- Attach the dividers to the top and bottom shelves, tacking them in place with finishing nails. Once again, do *not* glue them in place. And don't drive the nails all the way home; let the heads protrude.
- Make sure the case is square. Attach the backs to the top, ends, dividers, and bottom shelf with finishing nails and glue. Drive the nails home and set the heads.

When the backs are in place and you're certain the dividers and ends are all properly positioned, remove the protruding nails one at a time and replace them with flathead wood screws. Drive the screws up through the bottom shelf, countersinking the heads. Drive them down through the top, counterboring *and* countersinking the heads. Cover the heads of the top screws with wooden plugs, then sand the plugs flush with the surface. Sand all glue joints clean.

8

Join the front frame members. With a helper, turn the case over so it rests on its back. Lay the front frame members in place, and mark the positions of the middle front stiles on the top front rail. Remove the frame parts and cut the joinery. As shown in the *Front View,* the frame members are joined with wooden plates or "biscuits." You can also use dowels. Cut the slots for the biscuits with a plate joiner. Or, if you're doweling the parts together, drill dowel holes using a doweling jig to guide the bit.

9

Chamfer the edges of the front stiles. As shown in the *Front View, Side View,* and *Bookcase Joinery Detail,* the edges of the front stiles are chamfered. Cut these chamfers with a shaper or router, stopping each chamfer at both ends. Begin the chamfers on the front end stiles 4″ from the top, and stop them 5³/₄″ from the bottom, as shown in the *Side View;* begin the chamfers on the front middle stiles 4″ from the top, and stop them 2″ from the bottom. (See Figure 2.)

2/Rout the chamfers in the front stiles with a 45° chamfering bit. Stop each chamfer a few inches from each end.

10

Attach the face frame to the case. Finish sand the face frame members. Glue them to the top, ends, dividers, and bottom shelf, gluing the adjoining ends and edges together as you do so. Reinforce the glue joints with finishing nails. Set the heads of the nails, then cover the heads with putty.

11 Cut and install the sawtooth strips.

Measure inside the case to determine the length of the sawtooth strips; it may be necessary to adjust the dimensions in the Materials List. Cut the strips to size.

Lay out the teeth on *one* strip, as shown in the *Sawtooth Detail*. Stack four strips, with the marked strip on top. Tape the stack together, then cut the teeth in all four strips at once, using a saber saw or a band saw. Sand the sawed edges, then remove the tape. Use one of the strips from the first stack as a template to mark another strip, stack another four strips with the marked strip on top, and repeat until you have cut the strips for all the bays.

Keep each set of four strips together and use them in the same bay. This will ensure that the adjustable shelves in each bay will be level. Finish sand the strips, then attach them to the ends and dividers with glue and wire brads. Set the heads of the brads.

> **TRY THIS!** Use double-faced carpet tape to hold each stack together while you saw and sand it. This tape keeps the stack from shifting as you work.

12 Cut the shelf supports.

Measure the distance between the sawteeth, and make any necessary changes in the dimensions of the shelf supports. Cut and sand the supports using the same stacking technique used to make the sawtooth strips. Lay out the supports as shown in the *Shelf Support Detail,* then saw and sand a stack of them. Make two supports for each adjustable shelf.

13 Cut the adjustable shelves.

Measure the width of the bays, and make any necessary changes in the size of the adjustable shelves. Lay out each shelf as shown in the *Adjustable Shelf Layout,* and cut the notches with a band saw or saber saw. Sand the sawed edges.

14 Finish the shelving unit.

Finish sand the shelving supports and the adjustable shelves. Do any necessary touch-up sanding on the case, and apply a finish to the case, supports, and adjustable shelves. To keep the supports from sticking, avoid finishes that build up on the surface, such as varnish or shellac. Use a penetrating finish like tung oil.

When the finish dries, rub down the case with wax. Insert the shelf supports between the teeth wherever you want to hang a shelf. Then lay the adjustable shelves across the supports.

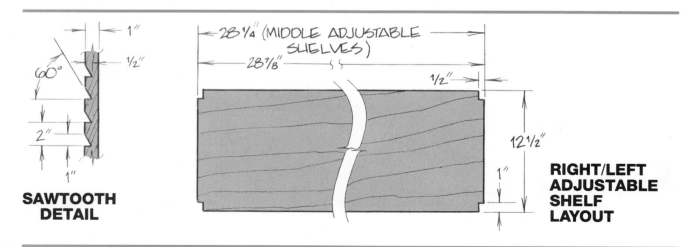

SAWTOOTH DETAIL

RIGHT/LEFT ADJUSTABLE SHELF LAYOUT

Chimney Shelves

In the northern states, carpenters and masons often placed the chimneys *inside* country houses. This helped to conserve heat. And it sometimes created narrow spaces between a massive fireplace and the corners of the room. To use these spaces, cabinetmakers invented several tall, narrow pieces of furniture. Among them were these "chimney shelves."

Chimney shelves can be easily expanded or contracted to fill the available space. The units shown are 48″ wide, 16″ deep, and 90″ tall. However, you can make them as wide, deep, or tall as you have room for. The "step" shelf is about 60″ high, to match the mantle over the fireplace. You can change this, too. Not all chimney shelves had steps, since not all fireplaces had mantles.

Finally, you can make these shelves as built-ins or stand-alone units. The chimney shelves shown are built-ins — they are fastened permanently to the wall on either side of the chimney. But each unit will stand by itself without being fastened in place — the design doesn't require the wall for support.

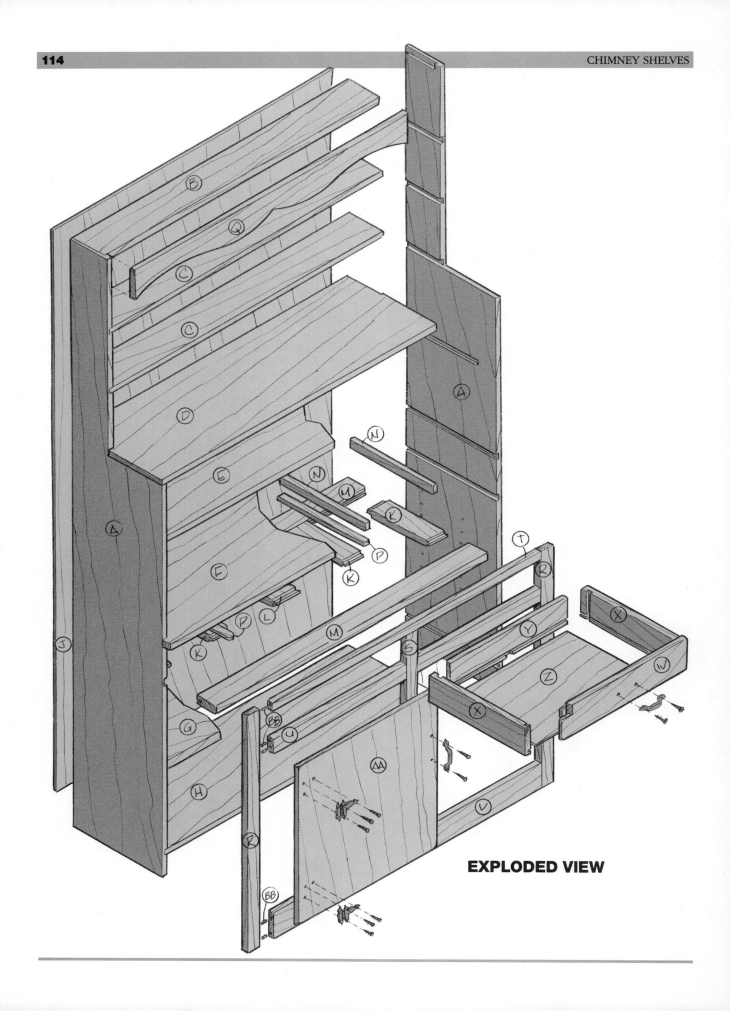

EXPLODED VIEW

Materials List

FINISHED DIMENSIONS

PARTS

For One Unit

A.	Sides (2)	$3/4'' \times 15^1/4'' \times 90''$
B.	Top	$3/4'' \times 5'' \times 47^1/4''$
C.	Top shelves (2)	$3/4'' \times 5^3/4'' \times 47^1/4''$
D.	Step shelf	$3/4'' \times 15'' \times 48''$
E.	Middle shelf	$3/4'' \times 12'' \times 47^1/4''$
F.	Counter	$3/4'' \times 16^1/2'' \times 48''$
G.	Adjustable shelf	$3/4'' \times 12'' \times 46^3/8''$
H.	Bottom	$3/4'' \times 15'' \times 47^1/4''$
J.	Back	$1/4'' \times 47^1/4'' \times 86^3/4''$
K.	Web frame outside stiles (4)	$3/4'' \times 3'' \times 9^3/4''$
L.	Web frame middle stile	$3/4'' \times 4'' \times 9^3/4''$
M.	Web frame rails (2)	$3/4'' \times 3'' \times 47^1/4''$
N.	Kickers (4)	$3/4'' \times 1^1/4'' \times 15''$
P.	Drawer guides (2)	$1/4'' \times 1'' \times 14^1/2''$
Q.	Valance	$3/4'' \times 4'' \times 46^1/2''$
R.	Face frame right/left stiles (2)	$3/4'' \times 2'' \times 35^1/4''$
S.	Face frame middle stile	$3/4'' \times 2'' \times 30''$
T.	Face frame top rail	$3/4'' \times 1^1/4'' \times 44''$
U.	Face frame middle rails (2)	$3/4'' \times 2'' \times 21''$
V.	Face frame bottom rail	$3/4'' \times 4'' \times 44''$
W.	Drawer fronts (2)	$3/4'' \times 4^{15}/16'' \times 21^5/8''$
X.	Drawer sides (4)	$3/4'' \times 4^3/16'' \times 15^1/2''$
Y.	Drawer backs (2)	$3/4'' \times 4^3/16'' \times 20^1/8''$
Z.	Drawer bottoms (2)	$1/4'' \times 14^5/8'' \times 20^1/8''$
AA.	Doors (2)	$3/4'' \times 21^5/8'' \times 24^3/8''$
BB.	Dowels (18)	$3/8''$ dia. $\times 2''$

HARDWARE

#8 x 1¼" Roundhead wood screws (12)
#8 Flat washers (12)
4d Finishing nails (½ lb.)
Drawer/door pulls and mounting screws (4)
Offset hinges and mounting screws (2 pair)
Door catches (2)
Pin-style shelving supports (4)

---

1 **Select the stock and cut the parts to size.** To build a single unit, as shown, you need about 80 board feet of cabinet-grade 4/4 (four-quarters) lumber, and one-and-one-half sheets (4' x 8' and 4' x 4') of ¼" cabinet-grade plywood. These shelves are made from pine, but you can use almost any species. For informal, utilitarian projects, country craftsmen typically used pine or poplar. For formal, elegant projects, they used mostly walnut, cherry, and maple.

Plane the stock to ¾" thick. Glue up stock edge to edge for the wide parts, such as the sides, counter, and step shelf. Cut the parts to the sizes shown in the Materials List, except the drawer and door parts. You must fit these to the assembled case. After cutting the case parts, resaw a scrap (less than a board foot) on a band saw and plane it to ¼" thick. Make the drawer guides from this thin stock.

---

2 **Cut the joinery in the sides.** The top, bottom, shelves, and back join the sides in dadoes and rabbets. Lay out the joinery as shown on the *Side Layout,* then cut the joints with a router or dado cutter. Square the blind ends of the top rabbet and middle shelf dado with a chisel.

TRY THIS! When routing dadoes and rabbets in wide boards, make a T-square jig to help guide the router. Use the short member (the cross of the "T") to square the jig with the edge of the board. Line up the dado with the layout lines in the jig, and clamp the jig to the board. Rout the dado, keeping the router pressed firmly against the long member.

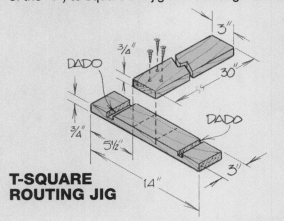

T-SQUARE ROUTING JIG

3 **Cut the web frame joinery.** The parts of the web frame are joined with tongues and grooves, as shown in the *Web Frame Joinery Detail.*

Using a table-mounted router or dado cutter, make $\frac{1}{4}$"-wide, $\frac{3}{8}$"-deep grooves in the inside edges of the web frame stiles. Then cut matching tongues in the rails.

4 **Drill the holes in the sides and kickers.** The adjustable shelf in the cupboard base rests on pin-style supports. These fit into $\frac{1}{4}$"-diameter, $\frac{1}{2}$"-deep holes in the sides. Lay out these holes as shown on the *Side Layout,* and drill them.

The kickers are mounted to the underside of the counter with screws. The heads of these screws are recessed in counterbores, as shown in the *Kicker Joinery Detail.* Drill the $\frac{5}{8}$"-diameter, $\frac{1}{2}$"-deep counterbores first, then drill $\frac{1}{8}$"-diameter pilot holes through the kickers, centered in the counterbores. Make three counterbores and pilot holes in each kicker. The spacing between the holes is not critical, but it should be fairly even.

5 **Cut the shapes of the sides, step shelf, counter, and valance.** Lay out the shapes of the sides, step shelf, and counter, as shown on the *Side Layout, Step Shelf Layout,* and *Counter Layout.* Cut these shapes with a saber saw or hand saw.

Enlarge the pattern for the valance, as shown in the *Front View,* and trace it on the stock. Cut out the valance with a band saw or saber saw.

Sand the sawed edges of the sides, step shelf, counter, and valance.

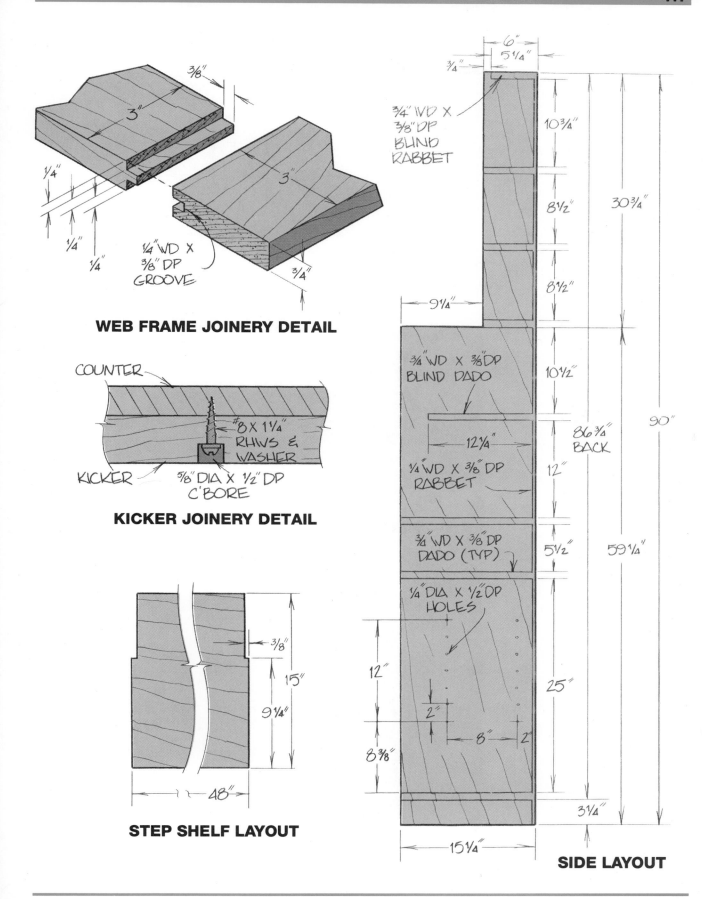

WEB FRAME JOINERY DETAIL

3⁄8″

3″

1⁄4″

1⁄4″

1⁄4″

3″

1⁄4″ WD X
3⁄8″ DP
GROOVE

3⁄4″

KICKER JOINERY DETAIL

COUNTER

#8 X 1 1⁄4″
RHWS &
WASHER

KICKER

5⁄8″ DIA X 1⁄2″ DP
C'BORE

STEP SHELF LAYOUT

3⁄8″

15″

9 1⁄4″

48″

SIDE LAYOUT

6″

5 1⁄4″

3⁄4″

3⁄4″ WD X
3⁄8″ DP
BLIND
RABBET

10 3⁄4″

30 3⁄4″

8 1⁄2″

8 1⁄2″

9 1⁄4″

3⁄4″ WD X 3⁄8″ DP
BLIND DADO

10 1⁄2″

90″

12 1⁄4″

86 3⁄4″
BACK

1⁄4″ WD X 3⁄8″ DP
RABBET

12″

3⁄4″ WD X 3⁄8″ DP
DADO (TYP)

5 1⁄2″

59 1⁄4″

1⁄4″ DIA X 1⁄2″ DP
HOLES

12″

25″

2″

8″

2″

8 3⁄8″

3 1⁄4″

15 1⁄4″

6 Assemble the case.

Assemble the case. Finish sand the parts of the case, then assemble them as follows:

- Assemble the web frame rails and stiles with glue.
- Glue the drawer guides to the web frame.
- Attach the kickers to the counter with screws (but *not* glue), as shown in the *Counter Layout*.
- Assemble the sides, top, top shelves, step shelf, middle shelf, counter, web frame, and bottom with glue. Do this with the parts lying horizontally, on their back edges. Make certain the case is square as you clamp it together. Nail the front portion of the step shelf to the sides, driving the nails down through the shelf and into the sides.

- Attach the valance to the top with glue, and nail it to the sides. Drive the nails through the sides and into the ends of the valance.
- Before these glue joints dry, turn the case over on its front edges. Attach the back with glue and finishing nails.

When the glue dries completely, sand the joints clean and flush. Set the heads of the nails and cover them with putty.

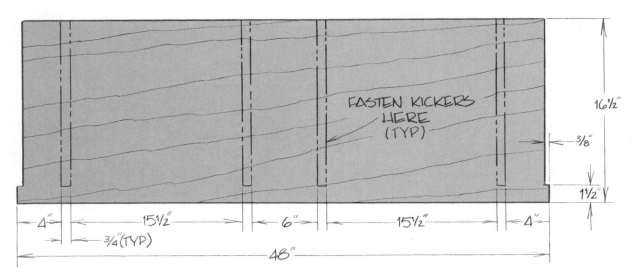

COUNTER LAYOUT

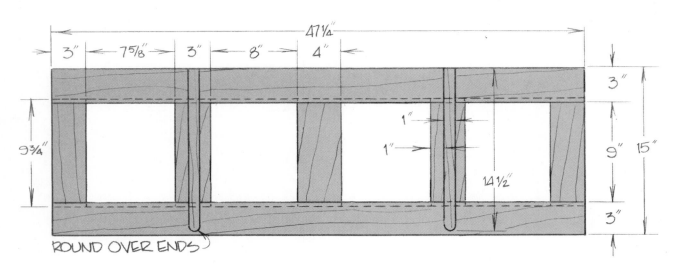

**WEB FRAME
LAYOUT**

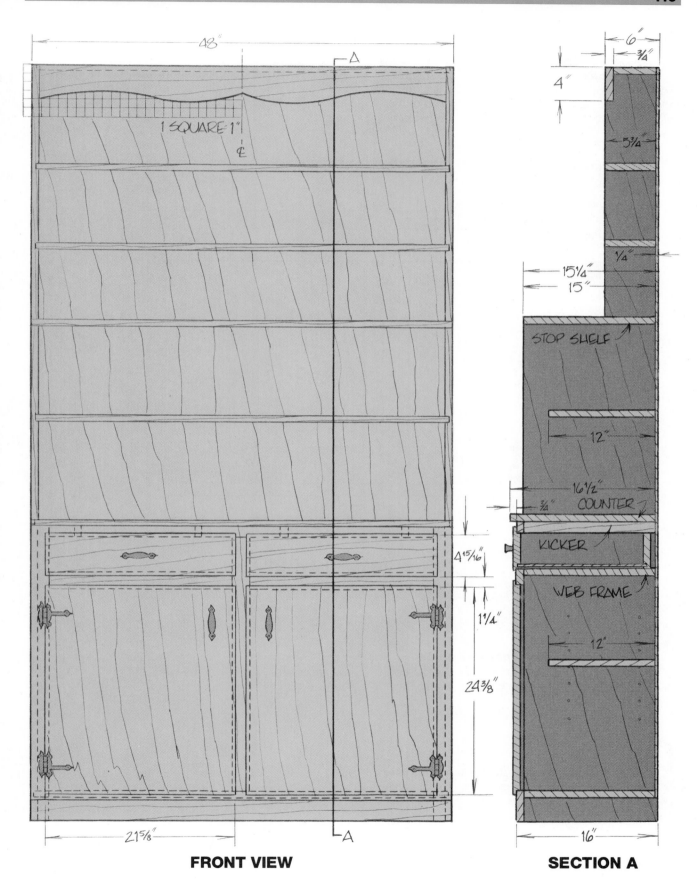

1 SQUARE 1"

48"

6"
¾"
4"
5¾"
¼"
15¼"
15"

STOP SHELF
12"
16½"
¾" COUNTER
KICKER
WEB FRAME
12"

4¹⁵⁄₁₆"
1¼"
24³⁄₈"
21⁵⁄₈"
16"

FRONT VIEW

SECTION A

7 **Assemble the face frame and attach it to the case.** Lay out the face frame members and mark the positions of the dowels. Using a doweling jig to guide the bit, drill ⅜″-diameter, 1″-deep dowel holes in the rails and stiles, as shown in the *Face Frame Layout*.

Finish sand the members, dry assemble them to check the fit, then assemble them with glue and dowels. Before the glue dries, glue the frame assembly to the case. After these parts dry, sand the joints clean and flush.

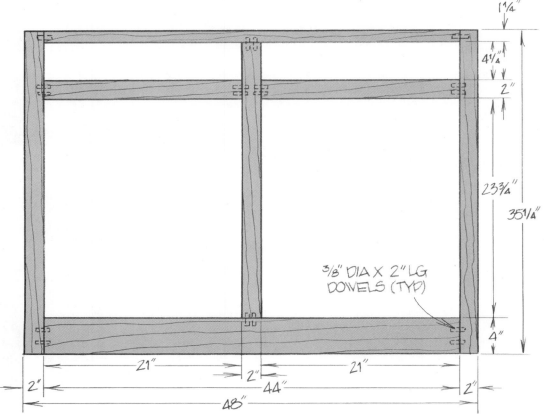

FACE FRAME LAYOUT

8 **Cut the doors and drawer parts.** Measure the openings in the case for the doors and drawers — they may have changed slightly from what is shown in the drawings. Adjust the dimensions as necessary, then cut the parts.

9 **Cut the lips on the doors and drawer fronts.** Both the doors and the drawers have lips overlapping the face frame members. To make these, cut ⅜″-wide, ⅜″-deep rabbets in the edges and ends of the parts, as shown in the *Door and Drawer Lip Profile*.

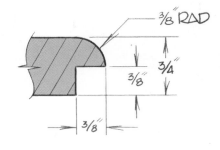

DOOR AND DRAWER LIP PROFILE

10

Cut the drawer joinery. Like the case, the parts of the drawers are assembled with simple joinery. Using a router or a dado cutter, make these dadoes and grooves:

- $3/4''$-wide, $3/8''$-deep dadoes in the sides to hold the drawer backs
- $1/4''$-wide, $3/8''$-deep grooves in the drawer fronts, sides, and backs to hold the bottoms
- $3/16''$-wide, $3/8''$-deep dadoes, $3/16''$ from the ends of the drawer sides
- $3/16''$-wide, $3/4''$-deep grooves in the ends of the drawer fronts (as measured from the cheek of the rabbet). This will create $3/16''$-wide tongues. Trim these tongues to $3/8''$ long, so they will interlock with the dadoes in the sides. (See Figures 1 through 3.)

2/Next, cut matching tenons and grooves in the ends of the drawer fronts. Each groove must be exactly $3/16''$ wide and $3/4''$ deep, creating $3/4''$-long tenons.

1/To make the lock joints that hold the drawer fronts to the sides, first cut a $3/16''$-wide, $3/8''$-deep dado, $3/16''$ from the front edge of each side. Make these dadoes in two passes, using an ordinary saw blade.

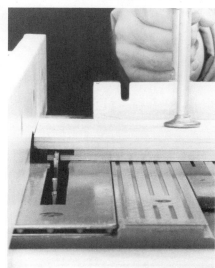

3/Finally, trim the tenons on the drawer fronts so they're $3/8''$ long.

11

Round over the door and drawer lips. With a router and a $3/8''$ quarter-round bit, round over the lips on the doors and drawer fronts. This is shown in the *Door and Drawer Lip Profile*. Sand the lips to remove mill marks.

12

Notch the drawer backs. The drawer backs are notched so they straddle the drawer guides. This keeps the drawers straight as you pull them in and out of the case. Cut these notches with a band saw or saber saw.

13 **Assemble and fit the drawers.** Finish sand the drawer parts, then assemble the fronts, sides, backs, and bottoms. Slide the bottoms into the grooves, but do *not* glue them in place. The other drawer parts are glued together, but the bottoms float in the grooves.

Let the glue dry, then sand the drawer joints clean. Attach drawer pulls to the fronts. Insert the drawers in the case, then slide them in and out several times. If they bind or seem tight, sand or plane a little stock from the sides and back until the drawers slide smoothly.

TRY THIS! Many cabinetmakers prefer to build drawers about 1/8″ oversize, then sand them to fit the case perfectly.

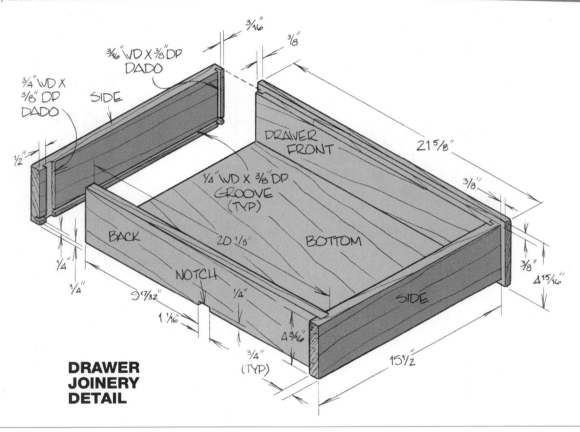

DRAWER JOINERY DETAIL

14 **Mount the doors.** Finish sand the doors and attach the door pulls. Mount the doors on the case with offset hinges. (These hinges are made especially for lipped doors.) Install door catches inside the case.

15 **Apply a finish.** Remove the doors and drawers from the case, then remove all the hardware from the doors and drawers, including the catches from inside the case. Finish sand the adjustable shelf, and do any necessary touch-up sanding to the case, doors, and drawers. Then apply a finish to the completed project. Be sure to coat all surfaces, inside and outside, except the drawer sides, backs, and bottoms.

After the finish dries, replace the doors, drawers, and hardware. Insert pin-style shelving supports in the holes inside the cupboard base, and rest the adjustable shelf on them.

Credits

About the Author: Nick Engler is a contributing editor to *American Woodworker* magazine and teaches cabinet-making at the University of Cincinnati in Ohio. This is his eighteenth book on woodworking.

Contributing Craftsmen and Craftswomen:

Nick Engler (Dish Dresser, Shaker Candle Ledge, Spoon and Plate Rack, Low Shelves, Hanging Corner Cupboard)

Mary Jane Favorite (Southwest *Repisa*, Santa Fe Wall Cupboard, Dish Dresser)

Carl G. Hill (Pie-Safe Bookcase)

Jim McCann (Clock Shelf)

Michael Surry (Chimney Shelves)

Note: Several of the projects in this book were built by craftsmen or craftswomen whose names have been erased by time. We regret that we cannot tell you who built them; we can only admire their craftsmanship. These pieces include the Tilt-Back Cabinet, Open High-boy, Child's Hutch, Bucket Bench, Whale-End Shelves, and Sawtooth Shelves.

The designs for the projects in this book (those attributed to a living designer/builder) are the copyrighted property of the craftsmen and craftswomen who made them. Readers are encouraged to reproduce these copyrighted projects for their personal use or for gifts. However, reproduction for sale or profit is forbidden by law.

Special Thanks To:
 Dave Arnold
 Richard and Susan Burman
 Mr. and Mrs. Douglas Crowell
 Mr. and Mrs. Nicholas Engler, Jr.
 Gordon Honeyman
 Joseph and Susan Rutkowski
 Wertz Hardware Store, West Milton, Ohio

Rodale Press, Inc., publishes AMERICAN WOODWORKER™, the magazine for the serious woodworking hobbyist. For information on how to order your subscription, write to AMERICAN WOODWORKER™, Emmaus, PA 18098.